Qu... books, vid... ...requests, and more, that help you nurture your faith and

Find your way Home.

At **www.QueenofPeaceMedia.com**
sign up for our newsletter to receive new content.

You can browse through
Queen of Peace Media's YouTube channel for help in safely navigating our tumultuous times.

To be notified of our new YouTube videos,
see www.youtube.com/c/queenofpeacemedia
or go to YouTube.com and search for Queen of
Peace Media, then click "Subscribe" and the
bell icon (top right of the screen).

Visit Us on Social Media. Like & Follow us!
Facebook: www.facebook.com/QueenofPeaceMedia
Instagram: www.instagram.com/QueenofPeaceMedia
Pinterest: www.pinterest.com/catholicvideos

i

ABOUT THE AUTHOR

Christine Watkins (www.ChristineWatkins.com) is an inspirational Catholic speaker and author. Her books include  the Catholic best-seller, *Full of Grace: Miraculous Stories of Healing and Conversion through Mary's Intercession*, and the highly acclaimed, #1 Amazon best-sellers: *The Warning: Testimonies and Prophecies of the Illumination of Conscience (El Aviso: Testimonios y Profecías sobre la Illuminación de Consciencia); Of Men and Mary: How Six Men Won the Greatest Battle of Their Lives (Hombres Junto a María: Así Vencieron Seis Hombres la Más Ardua Batalla de Sus Vidas);* and *Transfigured: The Patricia Sandoval Story (Transfigurada: La Historia de Patricia Sandoval).* Watkins authored *Winning the Battle for Your Soul: Jesus' Teachings through Marino Restrepo, a St. Paul for Our Century,* and *In Love with True Love: The Unforgettable Story of Sister Nicolina,* and the upcoming—if not already here—*Marie Julie Jahenny: Prophecies and Protection for the End Times.*

Mrs. Watkins has also reintroduced an ancient and powerful Marian Consecration to the world, which is resulting in extraordinary graces for parishes, groups, and people who go through it: *Mary's Mantle Consecration: A Spiritual Retreat for Heaven's Help,* with the accompanying *Mary's Mantle Consecration Prayer Journal (El Manto de María: Una Consacración Mariana para Obtener Ayuda Celestial y El Manto de María: Diario de Oración para la Consagración).* For details, see the end of this book.

Formerly an anti-Christian atheist living a life of sin, Watkins began a life of service to the Catholic Church after a miraculous healing from Jesus through Mary, which saved her from death. Her story can be found in the book, *Full of Grace.* Before her conversion, Watkins danced professionally with the San Francisco Ballet Company. Today, she has twenty years of experience as a keynote speaker, retreat leader, spiritual director, and counselor—with ten years working as a hospice grief counselor and another ten as a post-abortion healing director. Mrs. Watkins lives in Sacramento, California with her husband and three sons.

The author recognizes and gladly accepts that the final authority regarding the supernatural character of the locutions and heavenly messages in this book rests always and finally with the Magisterium of the Catholic Church.

Unless otherwise indicated, the Scripture texts used in this work are taken from *The New American Bible, Revised Edition (NABRE)* ©2011 by the Confraternity of Christian Doctrine, Washington, DC.

Names and places have been changed to protect the identity of the protagonists.

Books may be purchased in quantity by contacting the publisher directly at orders@queenofpeacemedia.com.

ISBN: 978-1-947701-12-0

She Who
Shows the
Way

Heaven's Messages for Our Turbulent Times

Christine Watkins

TABLE OF CONTENTS

INTRODUCTION

In the following pages are some of the most inspiring, remarkable, prophetic, and wise words of our day. They are words given from above to help a hurting and confused humanity pass safely across the tumultuous seas of our unprecedented times, and onto secure spiritual ground. God's children are seeking comfort and direction, and heaven is reaching down to provide them for us.

On October 7, 1992, the Feast of Our Lady of the Holy Rosary, Mother Mary and on occasion, her Son, began speaking to a Rosary prayer group in Northern Arizona, through interior locutions[1] given to one of its most unlikely members—a burly, six-foot-two, two hundred-fifty-pound, sailor-mouthed businessman named Walter, who had just experienced a profound conversion to the Catholic faith. Thus began the first of many weekly messages over the next three and a half years. The group's assigned leader, Mr. Gleeson, took great care to submit each message, as it came, to a priest for his review. As the revelations continued, he submitted them to ten other priests with advanced degrees in theology. All reported that they found the messages in keeping with

---

[1] **Locution**: an audible voice from heaven, heard interiorly. The Vatican biographies of both St. Teresa of Avila and St. Mother Teresa of Calcutta refer to their interior locutions, although Mother Teresa often preferred to remain private about them. Interior locutions have sometimes led to major religious movements. For example: the locutions received by Fr. Stefano Gobbi on May 8, 1972, at the Shrine of Our Lady of Fatima in Portugal led to the formation of the Marian Movement of Priests; and the worldwide, Church-sanctioned, lay association of the faithful, Direction for Our Times (www.directionforourtimes.org.), began when a secular Franciscan who goes by the pseudonym, Anne, a Lay Apostle, started to receive locutions in 2003.

Church teachings and containing nothing contrary to faith and morals. On July 27, 2020, Archbishop-Emeritus, Ramón C. Argüelles, STL, endorsed them with his full support.

Interior locutions are nothing new in the history of Catholicism. They are a form of private revelation, similar to an apparition; but rather than being seen, a locution is heard or received internally. Great Catholic saints, as well as unsuspecting, ordinary people, have received locutions throughout history. Because authentic locutions are direct revelations from heaven, they contain tremendous grace and power to effect great good in the hearts of mankind.

The prayer group started with a modest number of ten people who met in a member's home to say the Rosary. When the locutions began, their number grew quickly to around sixty, and they moved their gatherings to a church. During the three and a half years that the group gathered weekly, copious fruits and virtues—some of them extraordinary—grew and flourished among its members. They witnessed these changes within themselves and in one another. Some began attending Mass and the Sacrament of Reconciliation regularly. Others abandoned their worldly ambitions and careers and became Catholic teachers, ministers, and servants of the poor. Many witnessed to their children and grandchildren, husbands and wives, friends and strangers, who came into the Faith or drew closer to it. Conversions happened at an astounding rate. As the Spirit danced through the lives of the members, souls were set on fire, shaped into beacons for the Church and the world.

The prayer group called itself "The Cenacle of Mary's Children." The word "cenacle"—derived from the Latin word cēnāculum, "dining room"—is the name of the upper room in Jerusalem, where Jesus' apostles gathered in prayer with Mother Mary, and the Holy Spirit descended upon them in power. Over two thousand years later, Our Lady is renewing the call for her children to gather together with her in cenacles of prayer, such as this one, in preparation for a new outpouring of the Holy Spirit.

In her messages, Mary often shares her reason for coming to give messages to the faithful in these uncertain times, and she offers occasional glimpses into the future, as in this message from August 25, 1993:

> . . . My children, I pray for you daily that you do not lose your faith, a gift bestowed on you from the Father, Himself—a gift that allows you to see what others cannot, to hear what others cannot, and to feel what others cannot. I implore you to maintain your daily Rosaries, your renunciation of so many worldly pleasures, your patience and faith and perseverance. This faith you will need. It will become so important to you as we approach the "end of ends," the "time of times," that period for which I have been preparing you. I love you all, my children, and I leave you now with my blessings . . . and a kiss.

Today, the Mother of God wishes to share these messages with a vast number of her faithful children at a time when cherished truths of the Faith are vilified and love is growing cold. We are living in the end of an age, and as the world darkens, Our Mother and our Lord, as well, are giving us words encouragement and peace. They desire, through the remnant faithful, to ignite a network of lights that shine brightly across the globe through a dark storm—disciples who carry a message of joy, hope, and the unshakable certainty of God's ultimate victory.

If you sense a stirring in the private, most sacred recesses of your heart to respond to Our Lady's call, then take up this book in faith. Allow yourself to be wrapped in your Mother's tender embrace, absorbed in her words, and shaped into one of her great lights.

A NOTE ON PRIVATE REVELATION

There are purported "private revelations" that may appear to be heaven-sent, but are ultimately deceiving. To protect oneself against falsehood, "The authentic Christian approach to prophetic graces should always follow St. Paul's wise exhortations: "Do not quench the Spirit; do not despise prophecy," and "Test every spirit; retain what is good (1 Thessalonians 5:19-21)." Should the Church investigate a private revelation and deem it false, it should never be considered.

In St. Paul's first letter to the Corinthians, Chapter 12, he also describes the varieties of spiritual gifts given by the Holy Spirit to members of the Mystical Body of Christ for the benefit of the whole Body: wisdom, knowledge, faith, healing, miracles, prophecy, discernment of spirits, speaking in tongues, and interpretation of tongues are some of these gifts. St. Paul also says: ". . . he who prophesies speaks to men for edification, and encouragement, and consolation . . . he who prophesies edifies the Church" (1 Corinthians 14:3-4). Both Sacred Scripture and the Church's tradition speak of such gifts. Church teaching does allow individuals the freedom to believe in private revelations such as these, provided the fruits are good — in other words, if they bring people closer to God, His Holy Church and the Sacraments, if they are in keeping with the teachings of the magisterium of the Church, and are in accord with Sacred Tradition and Holy Scripture (public revelation).

THE STORY BEHIND THE MESSAGES

Aaron Gleeson used to be a man of little faith. His initial conversion into the rich depths of Catholicism was a gift from Our Lady of Medjugorje.[2] After a pilgrimage to this small town in Bosnia-Herzegovina, which changed him from a crestfallen and bitterly angry man to one filled with happiness and purpose, he began to share the messages that Our Lady of Medjugorje was giving to the world.

One of the people with whom Aaron shared Mary's messages was his old high-school friend and work colleague, Walter Schemel. Walter was a big, rugged, redheaded businessman of German ancestry, who dominated every conversation with his superior opinions and quartets of cuss words. Never was he overlooked in a crowd. He sported big boots and camouflage gear, toted hunting guns and six-packs of beer, hunted down deer and large beasts,

---

[2] The Catholic Church now allows diocesan-sponsored pilgrimages to Medjugorje. The Apostolic Visitor, Archbishop Henryk Hoser, is currently stationed in Medjugorje at the request of Pope Francis to be a representative of the Vatican at the shrine. He is charged with overseeing pastoral ministry to the scores of pilgrims who visit there and the construction of the shrine's expansion. In recent years, Medjugorje has been the third largest pilgrimage site in the world. The parish of Medjugorje keeps official documentation of many of the thousands of vocations and physician-verified healings that have occurred because of Medjugorje—the most important fruits being the countless conversions of heart because of pilgrimages and Our Lady's messages. The five main messages of Medjugorje are prayer, fasting, Eucharist, Confession, and Bible reading. At the conclusion of a Medjugorje press conference on April 5, 2017, Archbishop Hoser urged everyone to bring the light of Medjugorje "to the world that is sinking into darkness." He then stated, "You, my dear friends, should be the carriers of the joyful news. Say to the whole world that in Medjugorje we can find the light again!"[5] For more information, see www.MedjugorjeMiracles.com.

sped around town in a bright-red Porsche, and stuffed his mouth with chewing tobacco, which he transferred unceremoniously to the portable spittoon on his work desk.

Aaron had the privilege of seeing Walter five days a week. Walter's office was down the hall from his, where they worked as commercial real-estate brokers. Walter's co-workers would sneak out of the office just before noon to avoid having to endure his obnoxiously loud, braggadocious personality at lunch. Walter always knew more than others, being an authority on every subject. Those who ventured to express their opinions or knowledge would stand corrected. "Ah, that's so stupid," he'd say of people's cherished thoughts.

When it came to the Catholic faith, Walter's mockery would turn contemptuous. He was verbally abusive to his saintly, third-order Carmelite mother, and would often yank the rosary out of her hands while she was praying. "You're wasting your time!" he'd bark, and then tear her rosary to pieces.

Walter had strayed far from the roots he didn't know he had. He wasn't aware that the day of his birth, December 8, was the Feast of the Immaculate Conception; nor did he know that his maternal grandfather, Hermann, had held him up, as a newborn, to a statue of Our Lady and consecrated his life to her. Only later did he learn that Hermann, an imposing, red-headed German, who worked as a fireman for the city of Sacramento in the early 1900s, defended Catholicism as fiercely and passionately as Walter desecrated it. Once when a man spoke to Hermann with great disrespect toward the Blessed Virgin Mary, he threw him out of a second-story window. The "blasphemer" landed unharmed.

Despite Walter's jagged edges, Aaron got along with him swell. They had a shared history of rivalry against each other's all boys' Catholic high school football teams, each remembering their plays entirely differently: "I took you out!" . . . "No, I took you out!"

On the day that Aaron handed Walter a book about what was happening in Medjugorje, something extraordinary happened. Mr. Gleeson encouraged him to read Our Lady's messages, and Walter didn't laugh. He didn't poke fun at them. He quietly took the book and walked out of the office over to the Cathedral of the Blessed Sacrament, a couple blocks away. When he returned, he asked, "Do you have anything else I can read?" Surprised, handed him his copy of *The Poem of the Man God* by the mystic Maria Valtorta.

Three days passed and Walter didn't come into work. On the fourth day, he stepped into Aaron's office. Aaron looked up at him quizzically and asked, "Hey, where have you been?"

"I've been reading that book," said Walter. "I was so gripped by it that I couldn't put it down. I haven't slept." Walter ended up reading all four volumes of *The Poem of the Man God*—5,000 pages— in just a few weeks. It had taken Aaron a year. Highly intelligent and divinely motivated, Walter quickly devoured anything that Aaron handed to him. After poring over encyclicals of the popes, not to mention the entire Bible, Walter began to declare to all who would listen and all those who wouldn't, "This stuff is true!"

One day, barging into Aaron's office out of breath, Walter announced, "There's a decision I have to make in my life. I need to decide if I should consecrate my life to the Mother of God."

"That's great, Walter," Aaron responded, "but it's 9 a.m., and we have work to do. We can talk about that later."

"No, I need to make that decision right now," and Walter took off.

An hour later, he walked back into Aaron's office with a smile on his face and said, "I did it!"

"You did what?"

"I consecrated my life to Our Lady."

"What made you decide to do that?"

"I wanted to know if devotion to Mary was a real part of the Catholic faith or just something little old ladies did, so I went over to the Cathedral and asked God to give me a sign. When I knelt down in a pew, right in front of my eyes on the seat before me was a book. It was opened to a picture of Pope John Paul II, and he was kneeling in front of a statue of Fatima. Guess what the caption said: 'Pope John Paul II consecrates the world to Our Lady.' So if it's good enough for the pope, it's good enough for me."

Walter and Aaron began to attend Mass together daily at the Cathedral, during their lunch breaks. The transformation in Walter boggled Aaron who invited him to a book group in order to discuss *The Poem of the Man God*. Meanwhile, Walter had become just as opinionated about the Catholic faith as he'd been about everything else: "No," he'd chime in, "this is how it is . . ."

"Walter," Aaron would tease. "You just learned about that yesterday."

One day while Walter was driving home, an intense feeling in his chest, like a heartburn that didn't hurt, suddenly overwhelmed him. It was a sensation of pleasure so strong that he wondered if he would have a heart attack, and so he pulled off the freeway. Then he heard a voice that he believed was God the Father: "The Blessed Mother has chosen you to be used as an instrument of God. It will bring you great trials and great suffering. Are you willing to accept this?" Walter didn't know what this meant—only that he was being asked to be used somehow as God's instrument. Walter agreed.

Not long after that, Our Lady began to speak to him, especially after he received Holy Communion. Walter would hear her voice through interior locutions—in words as clear to him as his own—and she began to guide, shape, and teach him. Aaron would watch Walter closely at daily Mass. He'd see Walter return to his pew, kneel . . . and suddenly his head would bow down. Completely unaware of the world around him, he would listen attentively to the voice of the Mother of God and respond to her with his thoughts, in this miraculous form of conversation.

Once such conversation referenced Walter and Aaron's behavior. Early in Walter's formation, he and Aaron came across a mendicant wearing a patched and tattered brown robe cinctured with a rope belt. Curious and amused, they asked him why he was dressed this way, and he said he had given his life to God and chose to follow Christ by owning nothing and asking for nothing. If people gave him food, he ate. If not, he went without for a time. He said he lived only on providence, and only for Christ.

It seemed to Aaron and Walter that the guy was trying to draw attention to himself by dressing like St. Francis of Assisi. As they walked away, Walter scoffed, "What a nut job! He looks like a Looney Toon . . . What the heck is he doing?"—and so on.

An hour later, they went to Mass. After receiving Communion, Walter returned to the pew and knelt beside Aaron, his head bowed low. When he raised his eyes, his expression looked profoundly sad. "Our Lady just said to me, 'Because of your judgment of your brother, all the graces and merits you have thus far received in your life—all your treasure in heaven—has been transferred to him.'" Then Walter buried his face in his hands and wept from sincere remorse.

"Whoa!" Aaron thought to myself. "How many times have I judged others?"

On another occasion, Walter was worried about his family's safety and survival after he had heard rumors of America receiving a divine chastisement. During a locution, he asked her, "What should I do to prepare?"

In response, Our Lady asked him a question: "Which is a greater tragedy, that the entire world be destroyed, or one soul go to hell?"

He didn't know, so she gave him the answer: "If you add up all the hours of all the lives of all the people who have ever lived, who are alive today, and who will live in the future, they are but a dot on the scale of how long someone spends in hell. It is forever. Do not worry about physical chastisements. The loss of faith is what you need to be concerned about."

Meanwhile, their weekly book-sharing group had morphed into a Rosary prayer group. Word spread quickly among them that Walter, their most unlikely member, was now hearing from the Mother of God. What convinced people of his sincerity, more than anything, were the profound changes they witnessed in him: emerging qualities of gentleness, calmness, kindness, and peace.

Every Wednesday, at the Holy Cross convent chapel in town, the group members would kneel or sit cross-legged on the floor near the Tabernacle and pray the Rosary. One Wednesday, a Sister of Mercy looked over at Walter and said, "Maybe Our Lady wants to speak to our group. Do you think she would speak to us through you?"

"I will do whatever Our Lady asks me to do," Walter answered.

As they began, the nun prayed aloud, "Mother Mary, this prayer group is yours. We have dedicated this Rosary entirely to you and your intentions, and consecrated ourselves to you. Should you wish to speak with us, we are here to listen." They proceeded to say the Rosary, as usual. When it ended, they sat in silence for a couple of minutes. Then Walter, who had been sitting cross-legged on the floor, rose onto his knees unexpectedly in the middle of everyone, and began to speak:

> Dear children, it is I, your Mother. I am filled with joy at your presence, as you have gathered together here today to pray the Holy Rosary with such great devotion. Your prayers have made the Father very happy. There is very little in the world to make Him happy in these days, but your prayers today are bringing Him great joy. . .

The message continued, as everyone present stared at Walter and one another in awe.

> . . . Today marks the anniversary of a great victory in a battle won through the power of prayer. Your prayers are greatly needed at this time. Please pray especially for priests. . .

"What great victory is he—is she—talking about?" all wondered silently. The message lasted for about two minutes, while the group remained frozen in wonder. When it ended, Walter sat back down on the ground as though he had been transported to another time and place. Everyone stared at him, hesitant to say a word. Slowly, his awareness returned to the chapel and the present moment. When it did, he looked embarrassed. As a macho man, husband, father, and businessman, he hardly felt comfortable speaking the words of a gentle Mother—especially in public and in such an unusual manner.

The group members then rushed outside to look for pieces of paper in order to jot down what they had just heard. Using their collective memory, they pieced together the message and then looked up historical battles that happened on that same day, October 7. They discovered that the date marked the Feast of Our Lady of the Rosary, formerly known by its longer name, the Feast of Our Lady of Victory and Feast of the Holy Rosary. The feast commemorates the Battle of Lepanto, which happened off the coast of southwestern Greece in 1571. The vastly superior Turk forces were threatening Christian Europe. As the Turks advanced, Pope

Pius V called upon all of Christendom to pray the Rosary, and the Christian naval fleet was victorious. No one in the group had ever heard of Lepanto—not Aaron, not the Catholic sister, not Walter. Nor did they know that a battle could be won through the Rosary.

After that, Aaron made sure to bring a recorder to their prayer gathering, and Mother Mary continued to speak every Wednesday. She called the group her cenacle. Our Lady said she wanted them to be hidden and humble and to welcome those souls sent to them. But the group didn't want someone to join them off the street and turn pale at the sight of a "lumberjack" of a man getting on his knees with eyes closed and spouting eloquent paragraphs from a supernatural woman. They only invited a person after sharing the purpose of the cenacle, explaining the nature of locutions and their place in the history of the Church, and carefully vetting the person by understanding his or her interest. Slowly, the group began to grow, and Walter began receiving the support of Donald DeHaven, a deacon who ended up attending every cenacle and became Walter's spiritual director.

Many times, at the end of the group Rosary, Our Lady would give personal messages to individuals, and she never allowed those words of hers to be recorded. Walter would say, "Aaron, Our Lady said to turn the recorder off. It's private. It's only for them." Walter had no way of knowing if Aaron had already turned the tape player off or not, since his eyes were always closed. But Our Lady knew.

On one particular occasion, however, Mary made an exception. A beloved member of the group, a sweet and saintly woman named Lydia, had developed bone cancer, one of the most painful forms of cancer there is. At forty years old, she was dying. Her husband had left her over her illness, and she agonized over having to leave behind her two children. Her physical suffering was so great that she had no choice but to lay bedridden and motionless. Even people's footsteps, causing floor vibrations that moved her bed slightly, would send her into excruciating pain. She had blood coming out of her nose, and when caregivers tried to lift her off the bed, her arm broke. Yet, through all of it, she was joyful and filled with faith.

Since Lydia could no longer come to the cenacle, the core group of eight people decided to visit her in her home. Aaron happened to arrive before the others and asked her how she was. "I'm doing okay," she said, "but I'm really sad. Our Lady comes to me every night. She stands at the end of my bed and she cries. I think she cries because of my sins."

"No, Lydia." Aaron told her. "That doesn't sound right. Our Lady must be crying for a different reason." When everyone had arrived, they knelt around Lydia's bed and prayed the Rosary for her. All the while, Aaron wondered if Our Lady might have a message just for Lydia. When they finished saying the "Hail, Holy Queen," Walter said, "Aaron, Our Lady says you can record this."

"But I didn't bring the recorder," Aaron answered.

"She said you can record it."

"Wait!" Aaron remembered. "Maybe . . . my briefcase!" His recorder was in the next room. Mother Mary knew. So Aaron taped Our Lady's message, and in it, she gave to Lydia exquisite words of assurance and hope:

> . . .Your cross is heavy, my child, and it brings me to tears; but your strength, your power resides in my Son. I know this because I see my Son in you. I cry tears for your pain, and through these tears, so many will be saved. . .

This remained the only private message that Our Lady ever allowed the group to record. When Walter finished, Lydia darted her eyes at Walter and said with a smile, "Thanks, Brat. Ha, Mary calls you Brat!"

Walter's face flooded red and he whispered, "How did you know that?"

"Well, I heard her. She loves you very much."

"That's exactly what she calls me."

"It was so beautiful," Lydia continued, "the way her voice and your voice were intertwined when she spoke the message. You weren't repeating what she said. Your voice and hers were like two pieces of twine wound together. I could hear them independently, while they remained in unison." Walter confirmed that that was exactly how he heard and spoke his and Mary's voice within him. The message was a tremendous blessing to Lydia. Our Lady's words helped her to leave this world a couple of weeks later in a transcendent peace.

Jesus also gave messages to the prayer group, and He and His Mother used words that Their instrument would never have chosen, much less thought of. Walter knew well how important it was to convey Their words exactly as They said them, and he always took the greatest of care to make sure he wasn't being deceived in his locutions. He knew that the devil was forever prowling near, trying to infiltrate the messages or disrupt the harmony of the group. Before speaking, he was careful and precise—very orderly in his diligent testing of the spirit.

For example, one Wednesday as the Rosary came to an end, Aaron noticed that Walter was struggling internally, and it took more time than usual for him to speak. When the locution ended, Walter mentioned to Aaron in private what had happened. After the Rosary, a voice that sounded like Mary's had started to speak to him. As always, Walter tested the spirit. He asked the voice to praise Jesus. In every previous encounter, Mary had responded lovingly and effusively to this request. This time, however, the voice wouldn't answer and instead pressed him by saying, "My son, I need to speak to my children."

"Mary, please praise Jesus," he said.

The voice became more insistent: "My son, I need to speak to my children."

Finally, Walter objected: "No, I won't do it." Suddenly the voice changed and began to screech in anger, cursing him. When it finally stopped, Mary came and praised him for his obedience and discernment.

Greatly shaken and upset, Walter whispered to Aaron, "I was almost deceived."

During the prayer cenacle that evening, Aaron had noticed that the Tabernacle was open slightly. Peering inside it, he had seen that Jesus, in the form of Consecrated Hosts, was not there. "Look! The Tabernacle is empty," he pointed out to Walter. "We didn't have Christ fully present with us. Perhaps that is why Satan had more power to try to deceive you."

This small trial was only one of many far worse ones that Walter had to endure. God the Father had told Walter that being used as

His instrument would bring him great suffering. As word of Mary's presence at the cenacle spread, Walter watched the fruits of his obedience multiply, and he gained ever deeper wisdom and insight into the Church, faith, and theology—and persecution. Eventually the prayer group grew to seventy people and had to be moved to St. Elizabeth Church. People naturally started looking at Walter differently, either with skepticism or praise, and always under a microscope. Some doubted him; some called him a saint. He couldn't be just Walter anymore. The authenticity of the messages rested on his behavior. He could no longer tell his favorite jokes, glance at a pretty woman, or pound a few beers. As the cenacle grew, he felt increasingly awkward and self-conscious kneeling before the scrutinizing gaze of a growing number of people, and speaking words from the Queen of Heaven and Earth and the King of Kings.

When Mary first came to the prayer group, some people didn't join for the right reasons. One person wanted to incorporate other private messages from heaven. Another wanted to add the Divine Mercy Chaplet. One woman shuffled on her knees toward the Tabernacle when the Rosary ended, wailing, "I see Mary! I see Mary!" A Vietnam Vet who said they were all warriors for the Lord insisted that everyone pledge themselves to be a soldier of Our Lady while holding a sword in their hands. Another woman sat up in front of everyone, pulled out a ghetto blaster, and sang right along with it. The group became a free-for-all.

Then one day after the Rosary, Our Lady didn't come. She didn't come the following week, either; and she didn't come the week after that. Walter received the following message, when praying with Aaron in church: "You need to decide if this is my prayer group or yours. All prayer is good, and I will leave you to your prayer." Walter began to sob openly. He felt that he had let the Mother of God down.

Walter and Aaron convened a meeting of the core group of seven or eight people and decided to appoint a leader who would make executive decisions. They all pointed at Aaron. "But, I don't want to be in charge!" he protested. "Please let me just sit, pray, and listen. I don't want to have to confront anyone." But they had cast their vote and weren't retracting it.

At the following group, Aaron made an announcement: "I need to let you know that we're changing the format of the group. We're going to pray the Rosary, then Mary will come and speak to us, and we're not going to interject anything else. This is Our Lady's group, and this is what we're going to do. You are welcome to continue to come—all of you." Then he handed out a list of do's and don'ts for all the members.

The people causing trouble quickly noticed their behaviors on the "don'ts" list, which made Aaron a few enemies: "Who put you in charge?" . . . "This isn't your group." . . . "We can't just come and pray. We need to do acts of service, too" . . . etc.

"Everything you say is good," Aaron responded. "But this is what we're doing because this is Our Lady's prayer group."

The next week, Our Lady returned, and she began her message:

> Beautiful children of God, my children, I am so happy to speak with you this day. This short absence was necessary for your formation to purify you, to unite you, to make of you a beautiful jewel to adorn my Son for His greater glory. Unite your actions. Test them against the will of the Father. Look to their potential fruits. Do they bear dissention? Strife? Share with one another, and the Holy Spirit will guide.

Mary continued to come to the cenacle for another couple of years. The large group looked forward to her weekly visits, like young children anticipating their loving mother's embrace after a long time apart. She was and is the most kind of mothers. Never in the messages did she chastise. Never did she condemn. She spoke words of hope and encouragement, thanking her children for the little that they did for her, and preparing them to step boldly into the future.

In her journey with her cenacle, Our Lady let the group members know that her and her Son's messages would not last forever. On September 7, 1994, about half-way through her time of visitations, she told the group, "I wish you to know that soon I will not be with you in this way as often, and so I ask you to heed my words and pull close to my Son. I will show the way." About a year and a half later, on April 17, 1996, she gave them her last message.

As a result of Mother Mary's presence and messages to her cenacle in Arizona, Aaron, like many others, experienced a Mother's love as he never had before. To feel so deeply cherished by her and by Jesus inspired his heart to fall in love with the Lord and His teachings and to seek the narrow path. Aaron began to strive for holiness and reorient his entire life so that God was in the first place. Our Lady and Our Lord's messages also spurred him to learn all he could about Catholicism. He immersed himself in Scripture, papal encyclicals, books on the lives of the saints, spiritual classics, the documents of Vatican II. . . and eventually became a deacon in the Church.

Mary says in the messages that if her children open themselves to her words, God's light will fill them, and this light will be visible to others. This very thing happened to Aaron on innumerable occasions. People would comment at odd times and in unexpected places that they saw a "glow" or a "light" in him, of which he was not aware. One Saturday, when he was standing in line at a bagel store, a man behind him kept staring over Aaron's shoulder at his face. Aaron thought perhaps the man recognized him from somewhere. Finally, he tapped Aaron on the shoulder and said, "Excuse me. I know this is going to sound weird, but did you know that you are glowing?"

"Oh, I am?"

"What is it that you're doing?"

"Well, I just went to Confession and to Mass, and I feel wonderful inside, very much at peace."

The man stared at him, perplexed. Aaron sensed that a seed was planted.

Another interesting phenomenon would sometimes happen to members of the cenacle. When driving to the prayer group, an intensely powerful and pleasurable feeling would arise within them. When Aaron was taking Walter to the group one day, he gasped, "Wow! There's this strong, expansive sense of love, right in the middle of my chest!"

"I feel it, too!" exclaimed Walter. Mary had said that she would pray for the cenacle members to be united with her Spouse, the

Holy Spirit. This gift was a manifestation of her prayers. Through the grace of participating in the cenacle and living the messages, God has used Aaron, who considers himself a very imperfect individual, to convert to the Catholic faith several hundreds of people—and counting.

These life-changing words from Mother Mary and her Son, Jesus Christ, have remained hidden until now. When the locutions were happening, Walter worried greatly over the fate of their future until Our Lady said to him one day, "Do not concern yourself with what happens to the messages. It is nothing you need to worry about. I am entrusting them to the group's leader." From that moment on, Walter left them in Aaron's hands in complete trust.

In the year 2020, Aaron finally sensed Mary's call to publish her heavenly words. He knew that Our Mother had come to prepare not just her cenacle in Arizona, but all of her children to be apostles of the end times—bright stars in our changing climate. Her extraordinary messages were a gift to a few, and now it is time for them to be a gift for the world.

HOW TO READ THE MESSAGES

When reading these messages as an individual, it can be tempting to plough through them hurriedly or pore over a cluster at a time, as with any intriguing book. Going forward in this manner, however, would deprive your soul of their full benefit. Like Scripture, Our Lady's messages contain layers of meaning and are meant to be read prayerfully. A cursory read may obscure their deeper significance. If you are truly seeking union with the Almighty, if you wish to participate to the greatest extent in God's salvific work, please allow yourself time to rest in your Mother's and your Lord's words, one message at a time. Read each message slowly. Then perhaps read it again. Try to apply it to your daily life. Let it fill your soul with graces, with the holy strength and divine comfort that God wishes to give to you—personally.

FORMING A PRAYER GROUP

If you choose to read these messages in a weekly prayer group, the first cenacle members offer the following guidelines:

The group should have a respected, trusted, balanced, and prayerful individual as its leader. Members should be humble people who feel a call from the Blessed Mother to attend such a cenacle, and they should do the following:

Offer their entire lives to God, the Holy Trinity; consecrate themselves completely and without reservation to the Immaculate Heart of Mary; desire to know and love Jesus; convert their hearts, souls, and minds continually to God's will; become part of the Blessed Mother's plan for the salvation of souls; humbly obey and serve the true Magisterium of Holy Mother Church; courageously strive for holiness; study and learn the Roman Catholic Faith; passionately partake of the Sacraments (when they are available); lovingly adore Jesus in the Most Blessed Sacrament; recite the Holy Rosary daily; pray unceasingly; fast and offer small mortifications for the reparation of sins and the conversion of sinners; love others deeply; bear joyfully the burdens and crosses of life; and desire to become saints and apostles of these times.

BASIC GUIDELINES

In order to create the most conducive environment for prayer, members are to. . .

1) Recite an Act of Total Consecration to Mary. (See, for example, the Prayer of Childlike Consecration to Mary, which follows this section.)

2) Pray the Rosary slowly, in unison, in soft, gentle voices. Avoid praying in a rote and mechanical manner. Rather, pray in a way that offers each prayer humbly from the heart, honoring Mother Mary's presence among the group.

3) Arrive early, approximately ten minutes prior to beginning the Rosary, in order to prepare to enter more deeply into prayer by silently contemplating Our Lord.

4) Be seated quietly, making an effort to refrain from all conversation until after the Cenacle has concluded.

5) If meeting in a church or chapel, members should attempt to sit as near as possible to Our Lord in the

Tabernacle. This helps to promote unity in the prayer and greater fellowship among members. If meeting in a home, members should gather together in a sacred space free from distractions and interruptions.

6) Outside information, such as fliers, news, or announcements, should not be shared at the cenacle, unless approved by the leader, as this can lead to problems and division between members.

7) Strive for a bond of fellowship, mutual respect, sisterhood and brotherhood among members.

PRAYER OF CHILDLIKE CONSECRATION TO MARY

MODERATOR:

Oh, Holy Mother of God and our Mother, we love you, and we humbly invite you to be with us this day. We ask that you pray with us. Unite our prayers with yours to make of them a more perfect offering to your Son, Our Lord, Jesus Christ. Lead us to unite our wills to the Father. Help us to die to self for love of Him Who died for us. Lead us to attain a childlike simplicity of virtue, and a mature understanding of our Faith.

We present ourselves to you, worn and weak in our humanity, in the hope that you will wash us in the wellspring of your precious Son's abundant graces. Oh, what glorious cleansing!

We know that only the language of the soul can express the love you have for us, dear Mother, and this gives us the courage to say:

ALL:

We consecrate our whole beings to you completely and without reservation.

We desire to gain every indulgence and merit we can, as an offering to you.

We offer you all our prayers and this most Holy Rosary.

MODERATOR:

All this we freely give you, by the grace and merit of Jesus, to dispose of as you see fit for your holy intentions. Most Holy Mother, pray for our strength and endurance in times of trial or bounty. Lord, have mercy on us!

In the Name of the Father, and of the Son, and of the Holy Spirit. Amen.

THE 163 MESSAGES

MESSAGE FROM MARY
OCTOBER 7, 1992

Dear children, it is I, your Mother. I am filled with joy at your presence, as you have gathered together here today to pray the Holy Rosary with such great devotion.

Your prayers have made the Father very happy. There is very little in the world to make Him happy in these days, but your prayers today are bringing Him great joy.

Keep your eyes on Jesus, and follow Him as He shepherds you, His sheep, with His shepherd's staff. During these difficult times, His staff has been bent, but it will not break. You are His lambs, and He hears your cries. These bleats will bring many others to the flock.

Satan is especially active at this time. He will do all he can to draw you away. Today marks the anniversary of a great victory in a battle[3] won through the power of prayer. Your prayers are greatly needed at this time. Please pray especially for priests.

I will speak to each one of you individually in a special way in your hearts. Each of you has been given a special mission in God's plan. My Son and I are with you constantly. We are always present.

I leave you with my special blessing.

---

[3] October 7 is the feast day of Our Lady of the Rosary (formerly known as the Feast of Our Lady of Victory and Feast of the Holy Rosary) which commemorates the victory of the Christian naval fleet over the vastly superior Turk forces that threatened Christian Europe in the Battle of Lepanto in 1571. Pope Pius V called upon all of Christendom to pray the Rosary.

MESSAGE FROM JESUS
OCTOBER 14, 1992

My beloved children, My brothers and sisters, it is I, your Lord Jesus, speaking to you now. I am with you. . . I am with you now and am very happy. Your many sacrifices, your fasting, your foregoing pleasures, and your consecrations fill Me with much joy. There is much sadness in the world, much suffering. It brings many to wonder how I can come to them with joy and happiness in the midst of such suffering. It is the achieving of that joy in suffering that will make many of My children saints. All of you will be with Me in the presence of the Father. Sufferings and sadness will change to joy and happiness. I came to you as a holy example, as an example of how to travel the path that leads to the Father, and I gave you My Mother to help you along this path, and I gave you the Holy Bible. Read it and ponder its words in your hearts.

My children, your prayers for the Holy Father [Pope John Paul II, at that time][4] are most important. Continue them. Continue them with fervor. My Church on earth is entering a period of great trial. The Holy Father is not alone, without spiritual support. I am with him. I instruct him. He knows his mission, and he knows his sacrifices. Pray for My priests. Pray for those who abandon the Holy Father. There is so much need for prayer. For this you must pray.

My children, I come to you in this way to let you know that I am near, that I exist, that I truly love you. I am always with you when you invite Me. When your hearts respond to Me, I am there. Do not despair. Avoid temptation. Avoid those who challenge your beliefs. They do you harm, My children. Satan is very strong. He harms you with dissension, with confusion. He attacks with falsehoods, disputes, and

---

[4] Note: when Our Lady refers to the "Holy Father," the "Holy Vicar," the "Vicar of my Son," or the "Vicar of Christ," she is referring to Pope John Paul II, who was pope during the years 1992 to 1995, when these messages were given.

conflict. I tell you now, anyone who comes to you with falsehood and says that they know the Father's will is deceiving you. You must pray for them and take them into your hearts. You must love them. My children, pray, pray. Continue your prayers. Continue your sacrifices; but live in Me always.

If an unpleasant task comes your way, offer it up to Me. You must do this because it is the will of the Father. All understanding, all knowledge, and all wisdom are His, and He invites you to share these with Him. But you must sacrifice with joy and love, My children . . . and you are. I am most happy with all of you.

A tremendous work is about to begin. Countless souls can be saved, so you must all do your part. All of you will play important roles in what is to unfold, so support one another and listen to one another. You must help one another. If problems arise that appear to have no resolution, you must meet in prayer . . . meet in prayer. I know I have said this many times, in many places. I do so because I know many do not listen; but it is so important that they do! I understand you, My children. I lived among you. I know your strengths and weaknesses. All can be forgiven, but you must ask for forgiveness. I give you the Father's blessing. I will come to you often to prepare you. Be vigilant. Ask for My help. I love you all.

Good-bye, My children.

MESSAGE FROM MARY
OCTOBER 28, 1992

My children, come to me now. Send your hearts to me as little children. Run to me. I throw my arms about you. I give you all kisses of great joy. The Rosary today was most beautiful, my children, especially your consecration.[5] Your voices together in unity raise the spirits of heaven. Continue in this way. Do you see your hearts, my children, around me? They are the innocent little children you once were. I love you all so dearly. You are my little army of joy and love. You are beginning to shine. You will shine so that the whole world will see. Rest peacefully in my arms, my children. The love you share with one another you must take with you always.

The enemy is always near. He incites rebellion and jealousy. He incites division and confusion. When you are together in my arms, his weakness is evident. As I comfort you, smile and rejoice. His time is ending. His time is coming to a close. You all know, and you've seen the suffering he has caused. You've seen the suffering that the rebellion of man has caused.

What is this rebellion, my children? Can you feel this rebellion? It is a lack of love for the Father, a love for the Creator, a love that is manifest by obeying His Word and His Law. How many say they love the Father or they love my Son, but do not heed Their words? For these children, we all must pray, because they truly are children. They are in the dark . . . they are in the dark, my children. You all remember, as children, the fear of the dark, the desire for light. This is in all of you; this is in all of your hearts. Woe to those who don't seek the light, who purposely avoid the light, whose souls cling to despair and to shadow.

---

5 See page 23 for the words of consecration.

There are many lost children, like these, who will not know the joy of being in my arms. For all these lost children, pray, because many will be saved. Those who truly search, those who truly look with their hearts for my Son, in the end, will be found . . . will be saved. My Son is truly the Good Shepherd.

Hold me, my children. Cling tightly to me. The enemy's reign is about over. Many of you will witness the joyous return of my Son. Many of you here will witness the joyous return with me. His glory and power will be evident to all mankind. The time of peace and joy is afoot, my children. Rejoice! Rejoice, and go forth with love and with hope.

When I come to you in this way, I bring many graces. My instructions for you? Read the Gospel, my children. My Son speaks to you all there. All the instruction you need is there. He left those words out of love for you, a love that is incomparable, as is His Word. Search for Him there.

I will continue to come to you, my children, to give you support and love, to bring graces from heaven, to increase virtues in you. You will be my victorious army. Run along now, my children. Go and play. Go and work. Go about your business; but love one another. Deny the enemy inroads into your spirit.

I love you all so much. I see My Son smile.

MESSAGE FROM MARY

NOVEMBER 4, 1992

Hello, my children. I, your Mother, come to you today with a very special gift. I have asked Him to come to you to speak of prayer, and He has consented. The King of Kings and the Lord of Lords is in your presence. Bow your heads and offer up to Him your hearts.

MESSAGE FROM JESUS

Sons and daughters, it is I, your Lord Jesus, Who speaks to you now. I have come to you now at the request of My Mother to tell you about prayer. My children, when you pray, always pray for the virtue that opposes the challenge that you meet. If you feel despair, ask for the prayer of joy. When you feel challenged by pride, ask for the prayer of humility. When you feel challenged by the world and its complicated axioms and formulas, ask for the prayer of simplicity. When you feel anger, when you feel distress and hatred, ask for the prayer of love. It is written: those who ask shall receive.[6] It is through this asking and continuing to advance in your prayer life that I pour many graces upon you. As these graces flow, your strength increases, and you bear the burdens that I allow to be placed upon you. As you bear these burdens, you glorify Me, you glorify Me to the Father. In matters of generosity, can any one of you compare to the Father? So as you glorify Me, the bounteous way He will glorify you, you do not understand.

You must be simple, My children. In the Old Testament, the Father was not impressed with burnt offerings. It was

---

[6] Matthew 7:7-8

contrite hearts that He yearned for. So today, it's not complicated litanies and continuous prayers of words from stony hearts that I demand, but prayers of love and joy.

When you are dry, when you feel prayer difficult, this is the time that you ask for special graces, and you continue. You make Me joyful because it is through this trial that the graces flow and you see My light. When you see My light, it fills you; it fills your hearts. As it fills you, My children, it is seen by others . . . it is seen by others and affects them. This is part of the Father's plan. This is meant to be from the beginning of time, that My Spirit will fill My children and go out as a light to all nations. You, My children, will affect the people around you. You must have faith. You must have hope. These graces flow through Me, and all you have to do is ask for simplicity.

I love you all, My children, and I ask you to go forth and shine like lamps to My people. My Mother and I now go, and We leave you with Our peace.

MESSAGE FROM MARY
NOVEMBER 11, 1992

Dear children, it is I, your Mother, who speaks to you now. I go to each one of you, I hold your faces in my hands, I give you a kiss . . . a kiss that is a blessing from me this day. Behind each of you stands your guardian angel. In time of need, always remember them. When you were young and were told of your angels, you went to them often. I did this with you. As you grow older, the cares of life make you grow and change, and you sometimes forget. They support you in so many ways and have helped you over so many obstacles. Remember them.

I bring you joy. I bring you peace this day. This peace I offer you is being with the Father. Unless you are with the Father, there is no peace; and without peace, there is no happiness. Happiness is holiness. There is no separation of the two. Without holiness, no one can be truly happy.

Severe trials are ahead for all of you, my children. You will be tested in many different ways. The battle is raging in heaven, and the enemy is most unhappy with your prayers. They wound him, and his time is short. He is lashing back with all his fury. He will try you all in so many ways. You must hold fast to your faith. You must continue to pray.

Today I have brought someone special to speak with you. He has something to share.

MESSAGE FROM ST. MICHAEL THE ARCHANGEL

Glorious Heavenly Queen, I thank you for allowing me to speak with God's children. It is I, Michael the Archangel, who speaks to you now, children. I come to give you news of the battle, the battle raging as we speak. The enemy is defeated. He knows it now. He thrashes in agony. He tries to wound you all. He tests you all because of your prayers and your support. And I ask you this, I implore this of you: continue your prayers, continue them fervently—but continue them. And in your apostolate,[7] in your discussions with people, keep the Lord central and prayer central. Don't be trapped into long discourses and discussions about theology, about differences in religion. At this time, that trail is too long to follow and leads only to division. Promote the Lord, our God, and promote prayer, children. Keep these central. As you promote these, the enemy becomes weaker and weaker.

As our Holy Queen has stated, you will all be tested. You will be tested in different ways. In these tests, call on her and ask me for my help. Bow your heads and beg the Lord Jesus His protection. He will not let you down. These are glorious times we enter into. You will be at my side. The enemy's time draws close to an end. All of you will participate in the glories to be. But you must persevere.

I thank you now for listening, my children. Holy Mother, I beg leave.

MESSAGE FROM MARY

This is your Mother, children. Go in peace. My angel's words are spoken with strength and for your support—support I know you need, support you will get. In your consecrations to me, I remember your offerings. These offerings will not be wasted, my children. They will be used for the greater glory of God and so that you can obtain holiness—a holiness you so ardently desire.

Good-bye, my children. Go in peace.

---

[7] **Apostolate**: a work or mission accomplished on the Lord's behalf; work carried out by the non-ordained; vocation of the lay person

34

MESSAGE FROM MARY
NOVEMBER 18, 1992

Dear children, it is I, your Mother, who speaks to you now. Very soon I will no longer be coming to you in this fashion. But all of you . . . all of you will hear me in your hearts. Today my Son has some special words for you. You must prepare your hearts as He speaks to you through His servant.[8]

MESSAGE FROM JESUS

My children, it is I, your Lord, Who speaks to you now: the Lord who brought you the Word of the Father; your Savior; your Protector; the One to Whom you should always turn.

Tremendous change is afoot, My children . . . tremendous challenges for you. Soon it will seem the changes occurring in My Church will threaten its very existence. I'm here to reiterate: this will not be [the destruction of My Church]. Pray for your priests. Pray for your bishops. Pray for the Holy Father. Remain steadfast in your faith. Remember to turn to Me in these times of trial. . . and the trial will be great, My children. That is why My Mother has been appearing all over the world to reaffirm My existence, to renew faith and hope in hearts that were previously untouched—a testimony that many of you in this room can make.

We love you all so dearly and are so proud of your accomplishments to date. The adversary will not win. He is defeated now, but he is capable of causing much pain and anguish—pain and anguish that the Father allows. This is a mystery, My children. The answer will come in the fullness of

---

[8] Mary is referring to Walter, the man who began receiving these messages.

35

time, when you are all in glory. My Mother speaks the truth that soon We will not be appearing in this way. It is then that you will all hear Us in your hearts. We will touch you all.

It has been said that the works of God cannot be silenced. This has always been true. Try as he may, the adversary will not be successful. Hold steadfast, remain in prayer, support your priests and bishops. Be obedient. Continue your prayers and fasting, your charity towards others. Do not complain about priests and bishops. Leave them to Me. They are my charge. Prepare yourselves, My children. Prepare for great change. It will bring you all joy. The trials will be sweet, if you remain strong in your faith.

I love you all, and I leave you in prayer.

MESSAGE FROM MARY
DECEMBER 2, 1992

Open your hearts to understand these words. I come to you today as the Mother of Sorrows. In a little while, sooner than most think, my Son, symbolized by His Church on earth, will start its march to Calvary. I am in sorrow because so many of my children are taunting, throwing stones, blaspheming. The damage they do their souls distresses me. I can only help them through all your prayers. The time is not far off when, as my Son was hung from the cross, so will His Church be. If my children persevere in their faith and in their prayers, they will be united with me at the foot of this cross. But most of my children, like the apostles, will flee. They will flee out of fear. They will flee out of misunderstanding, and many will flee out of disgust and anguish, for they will feel that the Church has failed them, like the apostles felt.

In these times, my dear and loyal children who have persevered in prayer will be with me at the foot of this cross, and I will shelter them and protect them. Shortly after this, my Son will be in my arms. His Church will be held in my protective mantle, and my lost sheep will see their souls. The vision of their souls will cause fear, anguish, and sorrow in many, but it will be the fertile ground that will allow them to return in the completion of the victory of my Immaculate Heart.

It was my design that many of you were in attendance at the recent Peace Mass. I was there with you in joy. It was also part of my plan that my servant would speak so humbly from the heart in defense of the Holy Father, who is the Vicar of my Son.[9] Remember children, when you obey the Vicar of Christ, you are obeying Christ. When you dissent, when you argue, when you compete for attention with your worldly ambitions, it is in this way you are reacting also to my Son, the Christ and Savior of the universe.

My children, the Church is the body of my Son on earth, with the Holy Father as its head. When the head asks the hand or the foot to move, and the hand and the foot do not respond, this is paralysis. When the head asks the hand and the foot to be still, and the hand and the foot move, this is spasm. Both are destructive to the body. Both harm the body. A spiritual rot sets in, because at that point, the body is cut off from the head, and there is no feeling. A leprosy sets in that can only be cleansed by fire. This fire will be sent by the Father and will enlighten the souls of men.

These times, my children, come soon. Prayer is the answer. You must support your priests, support your bishops, be in union with the Holy Father. But only through love and sharing of my peace can you help those souls. The time for dissent and argument and division is past, my children. In argument and dissent, the enemy wins. At this point, what many of you consider righteousness accomplishes no good. Leave these problems to me. The Church will be in my arms.

I love you all, my children. Always remember that. Continue to pray, offer up your sacrifices, make the attempt to grow in the Spirit, and I will help you. Do not acknowledge the world. Acknowledge only the Father. Give all your love to Him. There are no other gods but the Father.

I leave you in peace, my children.

MESSAGE FROM MARY
DECEMBER 9, 1992

My children, come to me now. Lay your hearts before me. As your Mother, I come in this way to lead you to my Son. The love I have for all my children is so deep and so profound. . . only heaven can explain it. All of you are so special to me. The sacrifices you offer daily are pleasing to the Father. Gather around me, my children. Let me tell you the secrets of life: love the Father, love the Son, love your brothers and sisters—a mysterious secret, one that man has attempted to fathom for thousands of years. But it is the truth.

How do you achieve this love? Do you see all my lost children? They lock themselves out. They don't come around their Mother. In this way, I cannot share my love with them. My pleas go unanswered. It is because evil abounds in the world. But as the Father has promised, with the growth of evil comes the growth of graces, which is why I can come to you in this way.

I implore you, my children, pray the whole day. Fast, do penance, sacrifice, for as my Son has said, only in this way can certain demons be cast out,[10] and these are the demons that confront my children at this time. That is why I have implored prayer and fasting throughout the world, because only in this way can these demons be expunged from mankind. What do I mean by prayer throughout the day, my children? Think of my Son. That is all. In your work, think of Him. As you eat, think of Him beside you. Fill your heart with love. At times of temptation, consecrate yourself to me, offer your hearts to me. That is the prayer I require.

---

[10] When the disciples asked Jesus why they were unable to cast a demon out of a boy, certain biblical translations of Matthew 17:21 and Mark 9:29, such as in the King James Version, say: "And he said unto them, 'This kind can come forth by nothing, but by prayer and fasting.'"

Sacrifices? Simple, my children. . . usually things that draw you away from me and my Son . . . not your duties, but things of enjoyment. These are the things you can sacrifice. And after sacrifice, happiness will be yours—little sparks of happiness with each sacrifice, which will draw you closer to me, and my graces can flow.

Never forget, children, how much I love you. The sacrifices that I made, the suffering I endured as my Son was tortured, as He was whipped and disdained and spat upon— all of this suffering. I endured all this because it meant your salvation, children . . . each one of you! The learned, the intelligent, the leaders often apply this message to all mankind, but I tell you that my Son suffered all this for each of you . . . each of you! This is a mystery, my children. To fathom this mystery is to fathom the Father's love, which is boundless.

My children, bow your heads. My Son wishes to speak to you now.

MESSAGE FROM JESUS

Children of God, I honor and glorify My Mother. I ask each of you to heed her words for the salvation of your souls and those of many others.

MESSAGE FROM MARY
DECEMBER 16, 1992

My children, it is I, your Mother. I have, in my arms, the happy and smiling Infant Jesus. His childlike innocence and His beauty radiate on those who are around Him. No matter their feelings, no matter their sense of pride, His love dissolves all. I bring Him often to people and places in need of His infant love and the mercy that flows from it.

I'm so happy, my children, that all of you have assembled today to pray for and hope in my Son's coming. So soon your souls will be rewarded with His presence. He loves you all so much, and your prayers He holds so tenderly to His heart. He offers them to the Father. So many souls, so many of the Father's lost children are helped with your prayers. You must continue with fervor, with desire. Pray for all souls, even those you feel are lost. All of God's children are in need of His Mercy. His first coming was for just those.

My children, I am not far from my journey with my beloved spouse, Joseph. We walked and rode in the darkness. We suffered cold. We suffered humiliation. We suffered the arrogance and pride of the world. It was heaped upon our shoulders. But we continued on. We persevered in faith and in joy. What sustained me was the presence of my divine Son in my womb— this same and very real presence that He offers to all of His children.

Soon it will grow dark and cold for all of you on your journey. Like my sustenance was in my Son, so will yours be. Believe in the divine presence, my children. It will sustain you through all. Its graces will sanctify you, strengthen you, allow you to walk the journey. You must go, like my spouse, in pure faith, in love, and in humility—the humility to love all God's children, to avoid judgment, to avoid criticism.

My Son has given you all very special graces, many seeds that you are to plant. Be sparing and wise with these seeds. Pray as you plant them. Don't argue. Souls are converted from the heart, never from the head, my children. Remember this. And remember, as you get confused, as the times grow difficult and confusing, is it your heads that are confused or your hearts . . . your souls?

Through prayer, through fasting, through penance, through the willful bearing of the cross, my Son will pour out so many graces upon you. So persevere in heart and soul, so that no matter the confusion that enters your minds, you will stay with your hearts. I love you all, my children. I offer you my infant child. Caress Him and love Him with your hearts. See Him in your souls. Talk to Him often.

Good-bye, my children.

MESSAGE FROM MARY
DECEMBER 23, 1992

Dear children, it is I, your Mother, the Mother of Mercy, who speaks to you now. Your Rosary today was most beautiful and fitting these short days before the celebration of the Word become flesh. This occurred through the cooperation of myself with the Divine. The great redemptive act that began with Our Lord and Savior's birth will be completed in these end times, as once again, I cooperate in taking the charge that Our Lord and Savior has given me to prepare His way. My cenacles are growing rapidly, my children. They are springing up all over the world, like beautiful flowers—all of them with different missions, though their purpose be one with yours. You are my Son's apostles of these last times, and He pours out to you so many graces.

My many cenacles of prayer are like a beautiful plant with root and stem and leaf. It is enough, if you are a stem or a root, to be content with the mission that is asked of you. Be happy to let the leaf be the leaf or the root be the root. All of you, my children, in this cenacle are a beautiful flower waiting to bud. As the beautiful light of my Son warms you, you will open. This will allow the many bees that are sent to you to carry your dew to all those in desperate need. Your response to my Son's light is your humility, your true devotion and piety, your love for neighbor, your generosity, and above all, your obedience.

All men have choices to make in life. The most important choice is to turn to God. If you let my Son's light shine through you, all men, whether they believe or not, will be touched in a way that they will be made aware of the great choice they must make. That is my main work in preparing the way for my Son, because if men choose to turn just a little to my Son, graces will flow to them in abundance, and they will know true joy, and you will achieve great happiness in

43

being a part of this great plan. So rejoice in your trials, my children. Be happy in the crosses you bear, and I know they are many, for in this way you also participate in the great redemptive act of Our Lord that we are about to celebrate. [11]

I love you all, my children, and I leave you with my Son's peace.

---

[11] Christmas

MESSAGE FROM JESUS
DECEMBER 30, 1992

Beautiful children of God, it is I, your Lord Jesus, who speaks to you now. I come to you this day to speak of God's mercy and justice, an inseparable concept, not unlike the humanity and divinity that resides in My person—inseparable. Many people cannot understand these combinations of facets, and they confuse themselves and others by dividing them and analyzing them individually. I tell you, My children, people who do this are destined for confusion and are in grievous error. To understand these concepts and principles, you must have the gift of the Spirit, for without the Spirit, these are beyond human understanding.

God's love and mercy for you, My children, could not exist aside from His justice. It is God's justice that allows mercy, and mercy that compels justice. All the pains and suffering in the world, all the predicted chastisements, wars, and famines have been represented to you as God's anger, as His judgment, separate from mercy. I tell you, God loves His children and wishes no harm to any of them, but His justice allows these things to occur; events and sufferings caused by man's sin and his rejection of God.

An act of humility, an act of virtue, an act of divine love, like an act of sin, is a pebble thrown into the water. The ripples go on and on until their full action is dissipated. This is why there is a final judgment, My children. All your acts, good and bad, continue their effects on humanity until the end of time. You are judged upon death for the acts of your life, and you are shown the further actions that are compelled from the original action in the Last Judgment. So many of My children miss this important point. They look at the futility of some lives, the suffering, the pain, and they ask: "How could a just

God, how could a loving God, allow this to happen to the innocent?" But they don't look at themselves or their history.

My children, My dear children, continue your prayers, in your offerings, and in your works. Collect them like flowers. Offer them to My most sweet Mother. She will bring them to Me. I will hand them to the Father, and they will be used in the balance of justice and mercy.

All the sufferings and trials and torments you suffer, or you hear about, or you see . . . these are the effects, My children, of man's denial of God. And the effects will grow, as man's denial grows. These events, this information is given to you not for fear, not to breed in you a deep anxious concern for your futures, but to make you aware, so the signs given to you will help you in spiritual growth, and allow you to understand the mysteries as the Spirit dwells within you.

Go in peace now, My children. Continue in your prayer. Come to Me at the Mass. I love you all.

MESSAGE FROM MARY
JANUARY 5, 1993

Oh, my beautiful children, it is I, your Mother and the Mother of your Lord, who speaks with you this day. I greet you with joy and with all the love that a Holy Mother can bring to her children.

I ask you, this day, to contemplate my beautiful Son in the joy of His youth, growing strong and resplendent in the glory of God, increasing in human experience, living a life much like yours—and yet, a most divine mystery . . . the Truth that resided in Him, the glory of God Who He was, gaining in wisdom Who is Wisdom, gaining in strength Who is Almighty. The joy and strength of those days stand as a symbol for all time to the family and its place in God's plan.

I know, my children, many of you feel persecution. At times you come under attack, and the persecution seems unbearable. But know this, my children. If you bear them with humility, if you offer them to my Son for the salvation of souls, these trials truly redound to the greater glory of God and defeat the enemy and his minions—so many of them unwitting disciples, who challenge your faith and who attempt to lead you astray. Submissive humility, my children, is often the key. But so, at times, is strength, firmness of will, and resistance with your hearts and minds. Pray, my children, often for this.

Know that I am with you always and will lead you. Know that I am leading you most often when it seems the grayest to you. Have confidence in me, my children. Believe in our relationship.

I love you all so much, and I leave you with the blessing of comfort this day. May you praise God forever, my children.

Good-bye.

MESSAGE FROM MARY
JANUARY 13, 1993

Dearly beloved children, it is I, your Mother, who speaks to you now. I offer you the love and graces of the Father and my most Divine Son, your Lord and mine. I'm so happy with you this day—the beautiful Rosary you offered to me: my prayer, a prayer I offer to the Father on your behalf.

I know many of you are distraught about many things. Your concerns, your anxieties, they weigh you down. Many of you, this day, have been distracted in prayer. Do not feel guilt for this, my children. Offer this to the Father. He rejoices when you try to adapt your will to His. When you make the effort, He then gives you so many graces. Continue to pray, offer these difficulties up, even your inattentiveness.

My children, the glory that awaits you in heaven and the knowledge of this is now your cross to bear as children of God. Waiting for this is a trial, a trial that all the saints have had to endure. And I want all of you, my children, to be saints . . . to live the life of Christian virtue, to love your neighbor, to love your enemy, to exalt the Lord, your God Almighty, and to praise His Holy Name continually. These glories that will be bestowed upon you are impossible for you to understand, my children; but know in faith that they await you at the end of your journey. When the Lord calls you home, you will truly know my Son. You will see Him in His beauty, and you will rejoice in that vision through eternity.

Know this also, my children: the only way to the Father is through the Son, and the only way to the Son is from the pull of the Father. He pulls your souls to His light. He sends me to help you to see this light . . . the light for all men. Whether they believe or not, this choice all men will make.

I love you all, my children, so much. I pray for you daily. Believe me when I tell you I hear every one of your prayers.

My Son hears every one of your prayers. Sometimes you are like children who ask for things that are not in their best interests, so my Son weighs in the balance the good produced by answering your prayer directly and the good produced by responding to your prayer in ways you do not understand.

I love you all, and I leave you with my peace.

MESSAGE FROM ST. GABRIEL THE ARCHANGEL
JANUARY 20, 1993

Dear children, I am Gabriel. I am here to announce the presence of your Divine Savior. Bow your heads and open your hearts and offer them to Him, for He wishes to speak with you this day.

MESSAGE FROM JESUS

Sons and daughters of God, I bring to you this day the love of the Trinity, and I implore you to let it enter your souls. Open wide and allow this presence. I am so glad and so happy with the prayers you have offered this day. The beautiful way you sing to My Mother is showing her an honor that in every way exemplifies My call for an imitation of Me. Continue to honor My Mother in this way.

At this time, the enemy rages. He whips up violent storms. All you need do is rest secure on this Rock. To him, it is impregnable and unmoving. In his rage, he only dashes himself. His bones are crushed. But to those who love Me, it is a warm and loving heart. I ask you to reside in My loving and Sacred Heart. To do this is simple. Implore My Name, visit Me in your prayers, partake of the Sacraments; and also—and this is important, My children—come to My Heart through My Mother. For in this, Our hearts are joined, inseparable by the love from the Father. There is nothing more wretched in all the universe than a soul that rejects Him. I implore you to pray for those souls. Show them charity, beyond the charity that your human selves allow. I ask you through prayer to infuse your charity with mine. The effects of this will not be seen immediately—no, possibly not in your lifetime. But it continues. It goes on and on, My children.

So I ask you to go forth and proclaim boldly the Father's love. Do not be afraid. You have all seen and witnessed recently the enemy's attempts to confuse and to dismay. You have seen his control of your means of communication, how he can take two or three of your number and make a mockery out of it, a conflagration of My Church.[12]

Again I tell you, this Rock he cannot harm. I ask you to take this message into your hearts. Love and share with one another as I leave you now.

---

[12] Aaron had helped organize a Catholic event with a popular speaker, which drew over 1500 people. The media focused all their attention on the two or three protesters outside, giving a negative portrayal of the positive event.

MESSAGE FROM MARY
JANUARY 27, 1993

My dear children, today I come to you as the Mother of Consolation. I open my arms for you, to gather you in, console you, to share my Motherly love for you, and to share with you a great truth. Find shelter in my Immaculate Heart this day, and let me comfort you. I tell you, your prayers and voices, in sweet harmony from the heart, resonate at this moment in heaven still, and bring the angels to rejoice.

My children, man makes a great mistake. He conceives of God as a distant Creator, like a man who spins a top and walks away to watch it fall. I assure you, no act, no breath of wind, no tear, none of these exist without the assent of the Father. He is active in you. He is active around you. He never leaves you. How is it that men manifest their great error in their daily lives? They do this by the way they bear their burdens, their cross, without sharing it with my Son, Jesus, Who offered this. There is no consolation, my children, in your life's burdens without my Son, for indeed all these burdens are His. He carries them always, and He implores you to join with Him. That is why He said, "Pick up your cross and follow Me." [13] That is why He also said, "My burden is very light."[14]

Many of my Son's loved ones through the ages, beautiful children of God, have always amazed the world with their ability to bear any burden, suffer any pain, with immense joy. This is proof of the fulfillment of my Son's words, as a test for you, children—a visible test for you to apply to any sorrow, to any pain, to any burden—for if you are truly united with my Son in the bearing of this burden, you will find it

---

[13] Matthew 16:24; Mark 8:34; Luke 9:23
[14] Matthew 11:28

delightful and a joy, because you will have true knowledge of the benefits and the rewards awaiting you in your heavenly glory.

So when you feel yourselves in despair, and the pain at times feels to be unbearable, remember my Son's words, my children. Remember my words to you this day, because only there will you find solace, only there will you find the help you need. I know many of you find this hard to understand. You feel it has not worked for you. I promise you these graces will flow. In your next attendance at Mass, offer up your pains, your sufferings to the risen Eucharist, and await the blessings.

I love you all, my children, and I leave you now with my Son's peace. Glory to God! I love you all.

MESSAGE FROM MARY
FEBRUARY 3, 1993

Beautiful children of God, my children, it is I, your Mother, this day. I come to share my love with you, to gather you about me, to share my hope with you—the great hope I have in all of your salvation, in your meeting my Son face to face.

My children, we shall see you through, but you must cling to the Rock of my Son in His Church. You must seek refuge in His Sacred Heart because the devil rages. He whips up great storms that battle at your defenses, and I tell you that only in His heart is there true refuge, and a sublime way to His heart is through mine, my children. I couple my Mother's love with your tears and suffering, and I offer them to my Son. He moves toward me to take them with gladness and joy. He makes the journey so much easier for you, my children. You may struggle; you may strive to reach my Son. Many will make it. It is so much easier for my children if they know and come to understand that I am ready to take them there.

The enemy is so close, my children. He's so very near. He attacks from without. He attacks from within. Many will challenge your beliefs. Many will challenge the truths that have been revealed to you in your hearts and souls. All of you will be attacked at your weakest points.

Beware of those who fill you with fear in proclamation of my Son's words. Be leery of those who prophesy and make excuses. Equally, be leery of those who discount and disown all prophecy, for they all do you harm, my children—unwittingly, perhaps unknowingly, perhaps even without desire—but they do so as tools of the enemy. Do not be concerned about those who do not see or understand.

Do not be concerned about the size or growth of your prayer groups, your cenacles, or your families' understanding of your involvement. My message is small and meek, and it will grow of its own accord, in its own time, at its own pace. Have faith and confidence in your Lord. Have faith and confidence in me, as the Mediatrix of All Graces and as your benefactor in the submission of prayers to the Father.

I love you all, my children, and I implore you to keep these words in your hearts. Remember them in times of distress and loneliness and attack. Avoid those who wallow in self-pity, who manage to spread confusion out of their confusion. Keep to the straight and narrow path.

I leave you now with God's blessing. Good-bye, my children.

MESSAGE FROM MARY
FEBRUARY 10, 1993

My dear children, it is I, your Mother, who speaks to you now. I come to you this day to offer you the love of the Father, the love of my Son, and to tell you of my request that the Father send the Spirit this day to fill your hearts, to open your minds to understand my words.

Remember to consecrate yourselves to me.[15] Remember to do this often, especially in times of temptation. Your words of consecration send me to fly with my mantle of protection to keep you from harm's way.

My children, of special concern is attachments, attachments to worldly pleasures and possessions that keep you from the Father. But also, and especially damaging, are those of a spiritual nature. The reason, my children, is because they are so hard to detect. The devil can lay so many snares. Remember this: in any spiritual good or gift—be it prophecy, visions, be it gifts of understanding or feelings of the Spirit—rejoice in them, not in themselves, but in that they bring you to God and allow you to share His gifts with His children. This is what I wish to share with you this day.

You've heard it said, "Test the Spirit."[16] Test the spirit, my children. When in doubt, when confused, consecrate yourselves to me, because this is a temptation.

I love you all so much, and I come to you with these words to prepare you for your missions. All of you will have special and different missions to work on behalf of the Father. You will be given gifts. But to be prepared for these gifts and

---

[15] This day Walter arrived late and thus was unaware that the customary Act of Consecration to our Blessed Mother had been forgotten by those who began the prayer.
[16] 1 John 4:1

their proper use, your souls must be prepared. They must be refined.

I say again, my children, consecrate yourselves to me. Pray always. Offer your lives as a prayer. Offer the things you find difficult as a prayer. Come to my Son. Come to His Heart. Attend Mass as often as possible. Allow these heavenly graces to flow.

I love you all, my children. Good-bye.

MESSAGE FROM MARY
FEBRUARY 17, 1993

My beautiful children of God, it is your Mother, the Mother of your Jesus, who is with you this day. I thank you for your prayers, and I thank you for your beautiful singing. This day the angels in heaven joined you. Continue your consecrations to me, my children. With these, you offer your allegiance to my mission, and my mission is to lead you to my Son.

The path to my Son is narrow and difficult, and it becomes increasingly so, the further you journey. When you consecrate yourselves to me, it is in this way, with your "yes," that I can be your guide; and I will guide you to the highest spiritual perfection you can achieve in this life. This is a promise that I make as your Mother. Trust me. Believe. I am with you constantly.

At this time, the journey for many of you is rugged. You stumble and fall. This happens for many reasons, of which one of the most important is to remove pride. If the path were easy, if you constantly enjoyed success, it is natural to you to assume in your happiness that much of this power has been gained through your willingness. That is why, at times, through no fault of your own, great periods of dryness occur. You feel as if you have been abandoned. Your spirit reacts in different ways. Sometimes an increased longing for God and understanding of your own insignificance is readily felt. At other times, you easily and quickly fall back to those material things and worldly things that gave you false security in your past life. These are not necessarily steps, my children . . . not necessarily progress from one to the other. They interchange at times. But I promise you this: they will lessen as time goes by.

Have you noticed, even the most venial things you do at times upset you and concern you? You feel as if you have offended me or your Lord. Have you noticed a lessening of attachment to things you previously found fulfillment in, or believed you would find fulfillment in? Have you noticed an increasing awareness of those around you that suffer in ways they cannot see or even admit to, but you notice, my children? And this is not judgment. It's an awareness that comes from the Spirit. Do not feel you judge when you notice these things. Is it judgment to notice a man is starving? Is it judgment if you know that a man is filthy . . . needs cleaning? No, of course not, my children. As you continue on this path, your awareness of spiritual filth, of spiritual hunger, will become more obvious, and your compassion will build. This is a promise, children, I make to you as your Mother. If you consecrate yourselves to me, if you back up your "yes" with action, if you fervently desire to continue on this path to my Son, I promise you will arrive. I will bring you safely there.

You need strength for this journey. You need spiritual food for this journey. Partake of the Sacraments as often as you can. I love you all, and I leave you this day with my Son's peace and the gift of His Spirit. Let it warm your souls.

Good-bye.

MESSAGE FROM MARY
MARCH 3, 1993

My beautiful children, how I love you all. This is your holy Mother who speaks to you now in the quiet of the sanctuary. I come to tell you of the great graces that are being bestowed on you in this time of Lent, as you reflect upon the trials and sufferings of your beloved Lord, my Son, Jesus. I am so encouraged with your progress, and you fill me with such joy as you respond to my call. During this time of Lent, as you meditate upon my Son's trials and sufferings, as you offer up your penances and your periods bearing the heavy weight of the cross, I ask you, during these periods, to again think of my Son in the way you were instructed in an earlier discussion with you.

Your hearts are open to me, and because of this, the Son has allowed the graces of the Father to flow and to fill your hearts with a deep love and knowledge and awareness of His presence. This awareness of His presence is total prayer. And as you are filled with graces through your sacrifice, this awareness will become more manifest to you . . . a knowing awareness of the presence of your Lord. This awareness is not unlike the awareness you have of others in the room with you, yet you do not think of them at all times. You are simply aware of their presence. It is like this, my children. Words cannot truly and accurately describe the total import of what I tell you, but I assure you, as these graces unfold, you will experience all.

As you know, my children, as I have told you many times, the Church is entering a period of great trial. The wolf is loose in the sheepfold, and my sheep are scattered. But the Son has empowered me to shelter my sheep and to protect them, and the wolf has only his own doom to look forward to. Be effective witnesses of my love. By example, show the

60

faithful the true way of the cross and the true path to the Father. It is through your example and your witness that you are most effective as soldiers in my cohort. I know at times, you see with dismay the destruction that is occurring in the Church and in the lives around you. Bear up, my children. Bear up with confidence, for I tell you, the Lord's greatness is manifest in the small and the weak. The great and mighty are never used, my children. In the Old Testament, it is said that armies decrease in size, at the word of God, to win His battles for Him. This is an important concept, my children, as you see the apparent smallness of those who carry the torch of faith, for only the Spirit, only the most Holy Spirit, can truly convert souls. You are vessels through which His light can shine.

I love you all so much, and again I tell you of the joy with which my heart is filled at your progress. This makes my Son and I so happy. Continue on in your work.

I love you all, my children. Good-bye.

MESSAGE FROM ST. MICHAEL THE ARCHANGEL
MARCH 10, 1993

Chosen children of God, it is I, Michael the Archangel, who speaks to you now. I come to you as the sword and shield of God Almighty, as the protector of His children. Bow your heads and offer up your hearts. The Lord of Hosts, the Savior of the World, is in your midst, and He wishes to speak to you through His servant.

MESSAGE FROM JESUS

Children of God, it is I, your Lord Jesus, who speaks to you now, and I come to you this day for a very special purpose. These messages that you have received from My Mother, Myself, and other sources, are a very special grace and gift to all of you. They are for your instruction. They are to lead you on the path to holiness and to an understanding of the important mission that has been laid out before you. Please refer to them. Let them speak to your hearts.

My Mother, My most holy Mother, is a perfect example for you to follow. She is also My special gift to you, My children. She will continue to come to you often, especially in times of incredible burdens and stresses. She will come to hold your hands, to calm your spirits, and to fortify you with her strength. Because of your devotion and your prayers to the archangel, I have entrusted him with your special protection. He will defend you. He will always be present to protect you, truly, from the wickedness and snares of the devil.

I ask you also to deepen your commitment to your religious practices. Continue fervently in your prayers.

Receive the Sacraments as often as possible. Fast. Do penance. Perform works of charity. Offer prayers on behalf of humanity. My Mother will lead you. She will help you. She will guide you and direct you in the way to commit yourselves more closely to Me, to truly become one with Me, and hence, be capable of joining Me at My wedding feast. I love you, My children. My most holy Mother, whom I honor, is here to speak with you.

MESSAGE FROM MARY

My lovely children, I wish you to know the great honor bestowed upon you this day and the incredible graces which you have received. Renew your commitment often. Pray unceasingly by making your life a prayer. Follow where I lead. Offer your hearts to me, my children, so that I may swiftly carry them to my Son and to the Father. There is so much I could tell you, my children, so much I could share, but at this time I have been allowed to share with you a final truth for this period of your instruction. During this period of Lent, we prepare for the passion and death of my Son. I ask you all to listen closely and try to understand these words. My Son's passion and death were for each one of you. It's commonly referred to as "a death suffered for all," as "a sacrifice made for many." Though this is true, a central point is that it's a sacrifice and a death offered for each one of you. The terrible sufferings, the trials, and torments He endured were not just the total of all sufferings and sins on His shoulders. That suffering was equally strong for each of you individually. Hence, it's a debt that cannot be repaid by sufferings of your own. You cannot look upon your sufferings as repayment of the small part you contributed to my Son's. This point is so important, my children, because so many men, so many women, feel in a prideful way that through their sufferings or sacrifices, they have wiped the slate clean, they balanced the books. This is error, my children. It's a debt that can never be repaid. You must look with wonder and glory upon the saving Sacrifice of my Son. Be thankful for His forgiveness, and love Him all the days of your life.

I leave you now, my children. I love you all so much. St. Michael, protect them. I leave you with my Son's peace and immeasurable graces.

MESSAGE FROM JESUS
MARCH 17, 1993

Beautiful children of God, it is I, your Lord Jesus, Who speaks to you now. I bring you this day the blessings from the Trinity. I implore you to invoke the name of the Trinity often in your prayers.

You, My children, are to be My light in the world. You are being prepared and groomed for this mission. When you do your prayers and sacrifices, your fasting and your works of charity, you slowly and surely progress to the spiritual heights that will be required for this mission. I love you all so much, and with heavenly compassion, I help you to endure your crosses and bear your pains. Continue to offer them to Me. This pleases Me so.

In this time of Lent, My children, bear in mind the sufferings that I endured for all of mankind and for each of you. Imagine your own children, your own family—the ones you love the most, turning against you, vilifying you, torturing you, condemning you, and finally, committing the act of murder. Imagine enduring all this with humility, with the full knowledge that they would continue to do this throughout time . . . to each other and to your memory. This is a part of what I endured, part of the suffering that enveloped Me. But I did all this for you and would willingly do it again. The Father loves you so . . . that He would commit His only Son to suffer these deeds.

Many of My loved ones, in reparation, have suffered similar fates all over the world and will continue to do so, My children. Their sacrifices are worthy of the greatest glories in heaven. But you, My children . . . I ask of you the sacrifice of your love, your worship, your adoration. I ask of you the sacrifice of your living bodies and souls for the grand purpose that I've intended for you since the beginning of time. A time will come, filled with tremendous joy, and you will truly be beacons, My children.

Continue your pursuit: the possession of all the faculties required for this mission. Your spiritual exercises will lead you there. Trust in Me, My children. Have faith and hope in Me. All your crosses have purpose. They try you in the fires of suffering, of sacrifice, of giving—without consequence or concern for yourself. It is through these that you grow, that you mature.

Look to My Mother and her words. Heed them often. I leave you now, My children, with this last loving embrace, and I offer you My special blessings this day.

MESSAGE FROM MARY
MARCH 31, 1993

My beautiful children, I come to you today as the Mother of Mercy, that Divine Mercy, the Word of the Father, Who sacrificed all for you. Continue your prayers for unity and for the true peace that mankind so urgently needs . . .the peace that can only be found through my Son, Who is The Way and The Life.

There are many paths that can be taken. The one I request of you, my children, is the promotion of God's Church. I ask of you this mission, this work, as a holy work, destined in God's plan for the salvation of the world and the unity of His Church. Be my Son's lights and beacons. Share the Gospel— not by force of will, but by loving and gentle persuasion. Have faith in the charism of the Spirit with which you are endowed. Through you He touches souls in ways you will not see or understand.

My children, the times you live in are truly the times of my Son's mercy. Remember, the Father chastises those whom He loves. You are all being molded with spiritual fires that will allow you to shine in heaven for the greater glory of God. Please do not fear. Please do not be anxious about this great and important mission. Follow my Son's Church. It will not lead you astray, for my Son is truly in charge and is represented by His Vicar and all the bishops and priests in unity with him. Many will spread confusion. There will be great attempts to dishonor my Church, and I say "my Church" because, at this time, the Father and the Son have given me the mission to evangelize the world.

I love you all, my children. I know you will do your part. I love you all. . . and continue your powerful prayer. The prayers you offer are most pleasing to the Father, and with these prayers, He can warm even the coldest hearts. I leave you now to ponder my words, and I depart as I offer you my Son's blessing.

MESSAGE FROM MARY
APRIL 7, 1993

My beloved children, it is I, your Mother, who speaks to you now—the Mother of Divine Consolation. This is the week of my Son's Passion, my children. The glorious week that all that the prophets had foretold is fulfilled. Soon He starts His march towards Calvary, and I ask you, my children, to assemble your crosses and join Him on that day, for He will truly lighten your burdens, and you can participate with joy in the salvation of man.

Soon, my children, sooner than most think, the true Ark of the Covenant will be revealed. It will be seen by all men—the sign in the heavens to awaken and chastise their souls. My children, I am the true Ark of the Covenant,[17] and I offer you my protection and my help.

These times in which you live are eventful, and much will come to pass that has been prophesied. Stand firm. Maintain your faith and strength. Have hope and love my Son, Who has given so much for all of you.

I leave you now, my children, with my special blessing and grace.

---

[17] Revelation 11:19 and 12:1. Our Blessed Mother is identifying herself as the "Woman" in the Book of Revelation.

MESSAGE FROM MARY
APRIL 14, 1993

My dear children, it is the Mother of the Risen Lord who speaks to you now—the Chosen Vessel of God and the Ladder of Heaven. This day I wish to speak with you about the glorious time of my Church. When is this time? Soon, my children. Its flames will grow and be a light to all men: the Holy Church entrusted to me by special grace. During this time, it is about to increase the signs of love and hope and faith, for the world to see. It is paramount at this time that you pray for the priests and the hierarchy and the Holy Father, for unity among them is what my heart desires most.

My children, I speak of joy. I speak of happiness. But do not mistake them for the effects in the world, for the world goes its own direction, by its own path, and has you trapped in body until your death. Of this you have no control. So do not be concerned and confuse joy and happiness with how the world treats you. They are both very different.

Continue your attendance at Mass, as regularly as you can, for when you do, you participate in the most perfect prayer to the Father and in the Perpetual Sacrifice of Our Lord and Savior, Who died for you and for many.

The Mass was first prefigured by Cain and Abel.[18] Cain is the world, my children, and his works without faith were not accepted by the Father. But faithful Able, the loving servant of God and first martyr, who served God with love and with joy, offered a spotless lamb in sacrifice. For this, he is truly beloved of God. And I tell you this: how much more are all of you, my children, when you participate in the Sacrifice of the true Lamb of God. The power for salvation which you all participate in is immeasurable. And for many of you in the

---

[18] Genesis 4

world, as you are trapped, the "Cains" will revile you, will distrust you, will make your worldly existence a miserable and pathetic thing in their eyes. But persevere. Have hope and faith that I, your Mother, as the Ladder of Heaven, will be used as a tool by my Son to bring you to the Father, the source of all true joy and happiness and light.

I leave you now, my children, with my special graces and blessings.

MESSAGE FROM MARY
APRIL 21, 1993

My beautiful children, your Mother, the Mother of the Most Holy Church, the Mother of the Savior of the World, is here to speak with you.

Time is soon coming when you all will witness the marvelous rebirth and flowering of the faith. My work began from humble beginnings as I was sent by the Father and by my Son to rejuvenate and help those in most need, for nothing is sadder in all the universe than the loss of faith. Steadily and surely, members of my Son's flock have gathered to hear my words and to rejoice in their promise. All over the world, they are being prepared as lights and beacons, in union with all the priests and bishops who support the Vicar of Christ.[19] Slowly, but surely, a groundswell of faith is becoming evident. Faith is the glue. It is the bonding agent that makes the Church strong. The Church's humble beginnings were based on faith and grew because of faith's witness, and it is so today. Arguments about doctrine, empty discussions over history never convert hearts. Only faith does that, as a light to the world, as a magnet to those souls who are open to listen.

I tell you now, soon the angel will blow his trumpet.[20] My Son's sheep will hear the call. Their hearts will reflect and rejoice. They will abandon the cares of this world and reinvigorate and energize my Son's most beautiful Church. Oh, the joy of these days! The happiness and contemplation of these events fills my heart with joy, and I wish to share all of this with you, my children, to encourage you, so that you

---

19 Message given during the pontificate of Pope John Paul II

20 References to the angels blowing trumpets can be found in the Book of Revelation.

may recognize the signs and see them in your daily lives. The miraculous conversions, the healings, the change of hearts— all of these things are a witness to the truths I speak.

Fill your hearts with joy and love, my children. Though the paths are tough, and your times appear hard and without rest, I assure you, the joy you will eventually achieve is everlasting. I leave you, my children, with these words of encouragement because it is important for your missions to be lights of faith. Continue your fervent prayers. Continue your joyous exaltation. Continue your adoration of the Trinity. The cup is filling, my children.

I love you all, and I leave you now with my peace and my blessings.

MESSAGE FROM MARY
APRIL 28, 1993

Oh, my beautiful children of God, I come to you today as the Mother of Mercy and Love, and I wish to speak to you about faith and discernment. My children, with great graces come great challenges. In this world, for you, there is no way to avoid this combination.

In your consecrations to me, you have declared your desire for sainthood and your desire to receive many graces. I am so proud of you all because of the way you shoulder the burdens that go along with this. I know the enemy makes it most difficult. He truly does attack from within and from without. Your protection is to focus on my Son. You are truly in His presence. Your faith and love and hope have given you this. Forge straight ahead. Wipe the rain and the wind from your eyes. It cannot hurt you, for you are truly in my Son's arms. You feel the weather, you sense and see the weather, but I assure you, my children, it cannot harm you.

There is much falsehood in the world. There is terrible and deep falsehood buried and shrouded and hidden in Truth. Remember, the enemy is most skilled at this. Keep to your course. Do not waver. Understand he uses confusion— he uses confusion to breed despair. Again, I tell you to avoid this. Focus on my Son. Pray and fast, children. Certain demons that challenge your world are only defeated in this way. Discern by the fruits. Are the actions good? Are the reactions good? If they are, We are there. If they are not. . .

My children, faith is a grace from God, and grace is like the flowers of the field. As bees, you gather pollen. The industrious retire to their homes to make their honey. Others continue to flit from flower to flower; they endlessly gather pollen. The pollen is sensual graces, the graces that impact you, that give you instant fulfillment. But their true worth is their conversion into honey, a honey earned through industrious labor and work—the work of earning faith. Be receptive to these graces. Accept the pollen, but retire to your homes to make the joyous honey. Those of you who reject the pollen, remember, there is no way to make the honey without it. There are other graces, but you will miss these most beautiful ones.

I love you all, my children. I hold you all very close to my heart. In times of temptation, consecrate yourselves to me. Do this often during the day. When confusion sets in, when you are challenged, consecrate yourselves to me...consecrate yourselves to my Son. All your answers lie there, my children.

I leave you with my peace and my love and my maternal blessings.

MESSAGE FROM MARY
MAY 5, 1993

My most precious children of God, it is I, your Mother, who speaks with you this day. I come to you this day as the Mother of the Sacrificial Lamb of God—the Martyred Witness, the Son of Man, Who offered the great "All" for your redemption. Such was His love: a love the world tries to deny, but a love that the world cannot defeat.

At this time, the angels are poised with arrows of this great love to pierce the hearts of those chosen from the beginning of time to be sentinels for a decaying world, a world whose destiny is the grave. It is through this great and miraculous love, the love of the One True Deity, that man's salvation will be complete in his presentation to the heavenly hosts. The hearts that will change as this love fills you, my children—as it shines through you—are more than you can understand. You will see them touched, and you will know my words are true. Do not deny this great love!

Abandon yourselves to Him, my children, even as I had to do. The suffering I endured at His request was beyond what a mother can bear without the graces that accompanied this suffering. And I truly tell you that if you accept this great love, this great light that will fill your hearts with warmth, any worldly sadness that comes your way will be vanquished easily through your joy and your happiness in the Lord. And this effective witness will be seen by all and will touch them more than anything you can say. Many will even appear to reject. But the seed is planted, my children, and the Lord will water it. And at the proper time, the angels will pierce their hearts with this arrow of my Son's great and tremendous love. What love He had for you . . . to endure all your sins—all those sins of past generations beyond counting, and the terrible sins of those generations yet to come. It is beyond humanity's understanding. But in heaven, you will see and rejoice in the great glory it will bring you. Such is His love.

I assure you, my children, all of these graces will be bestowed upon you. No burden will be too heavy. No burden will be without reason. Remember, it is always darkest before the dawn, and you will achieve great, great joy, my children. Have faith. Follow and believe the teachings of the true Church. Support the Holy Father[21] with your whole might. Support those bishops and priests in union with him. Avoid discord with those who do not. Pray and offer sacrifice, my children. Leave them to me.

I love you all, and I leave you now to ponder my words. Good-bye, my children.

---

21 Message given during the pontificate of Pope John Paul II

MESSAGE FROM JESUS
MAY 12, 1993

Greetings, children. It is I, your Lord, Who speaks with you now. I come from the light, and I bring you the light. . . and that light is the love of God. I offer this love to all, but many do not accept. To accept this love, your soul must be prepared by doing three things:

- You must believe. You must believe in Me and My name, in the Trinity, in My presence, and in the Eucharistic miracle.
- My children, you must repent. You must be penitent of heart.
- And finally, you must ask. You must ask for God's graces.

Those are the three things, My children, that are so important, that allow your souls to accept My love. The love of God will then dwell in you, and the light of His vision will fill your souls with joy and understanding. You will not be able to contain this love. It will flow out to all My children. By your example and by your concern, they will see the truth. Be martyrs for the truth, My children, martyrs of love.

I have mentioned belief as being so important . . . in particular at this time, belief in the Eucharistic miracle, the greatest of all My earthly works of wonder. That is your shield from the enemy, My children, for upon receipt of the Blessed Eucharist—with a soul prepared to accept by its belief, by its penitence, and by asking for God's graces—you will be able to defend yourself from any attack of the enemy because you will be truly one with Me and with the Father: one body, a rock upon which the enemy dashes himself.

Today in the world, that great enemy is rearing its ugly head. Paganism,[22] believed to be almost exterminated by the victories of the saints, grows stronger every day. And with its many blasphemies, its many trials of My children, it strives to steal souls from Me. The signs of worship are obvious, My children. These worshippers deny Me, they deny the Father, and they deny My most holy law. They will grow, and they will get stronger; but not in a way that can harm you, My children.

Remember the joy in acceptance of My love and the protection that I offer you through the Blessed Eucharist. Enjoy this time together. Never separate. Stay in union, one with Me in the Father. I love you all, and I leave you with My special blessing and abundant graces for your open hearts.

---

[22] **Pagan**: a follower of a polytheistic religion; one who has little or no religion and who delights in sensual pleasures or material goods; an irreligious or hedonistic person.

MESSAGE FROM MARY
MAY 26, 1993

Dearest children, I wish to speak to you this day as the Mother of Holy Souls. The truest path to holiness and the only one accepted by the Father is through the Son, Our Lord Jesus Christ. His purpose for coming into the world was to provide this path, a path opened by His death on the Cross.

What propels you on this path? Only sanctifying grace, which is fortified and maintained by the Sacraments established by my Son and His Church. To efface the effects of the enemy, who is so very powerful and influential at this time, receive the Sacraments often and pray, because he darkens the path.

True holiness describes the possession of my Son's love, which is the light for the world. This light cannot be contained, however, because it only enters in full brilliance those souls made lucid. That is why the apostle said, "Show me faith, and I will show works."[23] This light is necessary to avoid stumbling.

I leave you with a gift and a request. The gift is God's blessing. The request is that all your prayers, even the formal, begin with a period of quiet for recollection to unite with me in contemplation of my Son. Think of His wounds and His Sacrifice, His joy in your salvation, or His limitless beauty. Be with Him, talk with Him about your concerns, be aware of His presence. End all prayer the same way. Will you do this for me? Don't be concerned about distractions, an inability to concentrate, or lack of imagination, because that is when Our Lord is working most in you.

---

[23] The apostle James (James 2:18)

If you earnestly continue your efforts, I give you my Motherly promise that you will reach the mountaintop so ardently desired, and as you ascend, your vision and understanding of the vistas of God will increase.

Thank you so much for your prayers, your love, and your offered suffering. Good-bye, my children.

MESSAGE FROM MARY
JUNE 2, 1993

My beautiful children, it is I, your Mother, who speaks with you now. I ask you to gather round your hearts so that I may fill them with my maternal blessing and prepare them to receive the love and light of my Son.

Love between the Father and the Son has existed since the beginning of all creation and before. That love *is* God. It is the Holy Spirit, Who looks to fill your souls, to find them pure, and to radiate out to all those who love my Son's Holy Name. Only the demons and those despotic in nature refuse this grace and blessing. Their hearts are hardened because the Spirit conflicts and competes with their own selfish pride, the pride of self, which is the ultimate weapon of the enemy, Satan and his cohort.

The demonic have not seen God. That is their fate for all eternity. But there is hope for all who live and breathe, despite their blasphemies, despite their hatred. You, my children, must learn to love them. It is through your beautiful hearts that the Spirit can touch those so hardened with stone. It is true you will not be successful in all cases. But who among you can tell which heart will soften and which will remain hard and calloused? Only the Father in heaven knows this. This is why it is so important for you to put aside your conflicts, your differences, your ambitions, your desires for recognition. Find what's important for all of you. Be concerned with those around you. Do not force your will upon others. Souls have their own flights, their own means to achieve grace. Do not cage them. Do not force compliance. Ask. Share. Love. Do these things in my Son's Name, and your reward will be most great in heaven. Do all in my Son's Name.

Though you despise the world, love those souls trapped in it. Live in the world with joy and compassion. Face obstacles with trust and confidence . . . and with bravery. My Son is always with you. He died for you. Would He leave you alone?

I leave you now, my children, with these last words. It is time to begin your pattern of fasting. The Easter season has ended. It is time to prepare for my Son's glorious coming. But I implore you to fast from the heart. Do not discuss it. Keep it to yourself. Be chaste in body and in spirit. In this way you will be most effective as witnesses.

Good-bye, my children.

MESSAGE FROM MARY
JUNE 16, 1993

Beautiful children of God, it is I, your Mother, who speaks with you this day. I offer you and bring you the love of the Father, and of the Son, and of the Holy Spirit.

I ask you to continue always your prayer as fervently as you have done this day. You battle against distractions and confusion with such power and strength. This is evidence of the great graces that flow from your perseverance. I am always near. My Son is always near. Start your prayers in gentle conversation with Us, for We are meek and humble of heart. Tell my Son constantly how much you love Him. Thank Him for His suffering. Hold His wounded hands and offer yourselves to Him. Nothing pleases Him more.

Very soon now, my Son's Vicar will come into your land on a very important mission.[24] The disciples of strife and anger will do all they can to disturb and incite. I implore you, my children, until and through the time of his coming, to pray for him and his mission. Unite your wills to the Father by supporting him with all your hearts, all your minds and all your strength. To be obedient is good, but to support him in this way is fundamental and so very important. He is the Vicar of my Son and does His bidding. *Please* listen to him, my children. Hear his words, understand, and support. He needs your love. There are so many pressures of the world being brought to bear, so many cultures challenging the Church. I *implore* you to pray for him.

Much anger in the world today exists because of my Son's Vicar— some of it suppressed, some of it open. Anger, my children, is the work of the enemy. It is when you are angry that you are closest to his domain. When you feel angry, when

---

[24] Referring to Pope John Paul II's trip to Denver for World Youth Day

it's uncontrollable, just say my name, and I will come to you and support you. If you know or are aware of any behavior of yours that incites anger in others, please pray, call to me, say my name, and I will come to you to help you to avoid the behavior that causes such anger. For even if you are in the right, even if you feel righteous in your desires to continue in such way, offer this to me and to my Son, for the rewards in heaven will be great for those of you who are meek and humble of heart. Anger is not part of heaven. There is only love and endless peace. That is why I call you to unite your wills to the Father, because in this way, anger and hatred, distrust and envy, will be left behind. Let Satan and his supporters enjoy such a bitter feast. I promise you much better, my children.

I love you all. I leave you with abundant graces and my Motherly blessing. Good-bye, my children.

MESSAGE FROM MARY
JUNE 23, 1993

My beautiful children, it is I, your Mother, who speaks with you now, and I tell you, this day you have pleased me very much with the way you prayed the most Holy Rosary. I am so happy, so delighted with your attentiveness and your understanding of the Mysteries. These Mysteries [Joyful] contain what is required of you in this life to be with my Son. They outline your purpose, my children. They are the reason for your existence.

The Sorrowful Mysteries entail my Son's purpose, His primary reason for coming into the world as man—the only man born with the purpose of dying for the salvation of the world. . . and the Glorious Mysteries—unification of all these principles. They are aptly titled "Glorious" because in them are all the glories that will be attained by all the children of God. My salvation came from my Son, together with the Father and the Holy Spirit. He is the First Cause, and of Him there was no cause.

The Church teaches love, humility, suffrage, and joy. There are many souls in the world who cannot combine these. Humility and suffering they find distasteful, and their primary reason for rejecting my Son's Church. It is man's humility, his unworthiness, his uselessness in relation to God's need, that the Church points out. God needs nothing, my children. In Him is all perfection. He does not need your love, rather He asks for it and requires it of you. Through faith, love increases. Through love, faith increases. He acts in many souls in many ways, but He does not harm the independence of the soul. The will maintains its independence, and it is because of this that His actions on souls and their reactions must be judged in the light of His Holy Church.

I love you all, my children, and I leave now with a request of you to pray from your hearts, to offer them to me so that I may console and caress them with my Motherly love and lead you to my Son, where you will find all consolation. It is the only direction you may go, my children, to find this.

I love you, and I leave you now.

MESSAGE FROM MARY
JUNE 30, 1993

My children, it is I, your Mother, who speaks with you now. I am so pleased with your prayers, your loving adoration of my Son. Continue to pray in this way. Oh, to see your formation, your development as children of God. It is so pleasing. My Son is so happy.

Avoid pride, my children. Avoid the prayers of those who, with false thanks, consider themselves superior to others in their spirituality, in their knowledge. Rather, pray like the poor woman who, in her poverty, gave the last that she had.[25] Your daily falls, your stumblings, and your sins are examples of your spiritual poverty. It is these that I ask you to offer to my Son daily, for in this way, you please Him most. I assure you, my children, that if you continue in this way, you will be led to unity with the Father in your permanent homeland. It is in this that your destiny, your glory, and your dignity reside.

Consider the Cross, my children, and the Sacrifice my Son made for all men. Consider it daily because it is a symbol of the cross each of you must bear in your own way. Pray for joy and humility. Pray for my Son's Church as it enters its period of severe trial. The servant is not greater than the master, and the master of the Church is my Son.

I love you all so much, my children. My Son offers you all His blessings and the graces you need to continue on in your mission. Good-bye, my children.

---

[25] Mark 12:41-44

MESSAGE FROM MARY
JULY 6, 1993

My beautiful and loving children, it is I, your Mother, who speaks with you now. I wish to thank you for the beautiful Rosary that you offered to me for my purposes. It will be put to good use. Some day you will see that use. I came to you during the Rosary. You felt my presence. I have been present since in this special way, as a gift for all of your preparation—for the importance you place on it is the importance *I* place on it, my children.

What a beautiful example you will be: a little holy family. All your troubles and all your trials will pale to insignificance very soon, my children. A great joy awaits you. There is much you would like to know right now. I know it. I see your hearts. Be patient a little longer. Grow in your love and in your sharing. Let that love and forgiveness swell inside you, until it's a joy for all to see.

You will be apostles of my Son's love; and now is a time of preparation. Sometimes you wonder if this is a time, if this is a place, for little ones. This is of no concern, my children. Soon the world will see my love, and it will shine in children like you. Jesus loves all the little ones. He loves you all so much. What He offered, what He carried, no one understands, no one, but the Mother . . . no one but the Mother.

I thank you, children. I thank you for your faith and your support. I will be your grace and your shield. You will bend, but not break, and you will be a great support for my Son's Church. All your Rosaries, all your prayers, all your acts of adoration I hold to my heart. They are very precious. And at the proper time, I always give them to my Son as a request, with intercession for you and for those you pray for. I promise you healing for all those souls for which you say Rosaries.

I love you, my children, and I leave you now with all my love and with special graces from my Son, Who lives inside you. Good-bye, my children.

MESSAGE FROM MARY
JULY 21, 1993

Beautiful children of God, my children, I am so happy to speak with you this day. This short absence[26] was necessary for your formation to purify you, to unite you, to make of you a beautiful jewel to adorn my Son for His greater glory. Unite your actions. Test them against the will of the Father. Look to their potential fruits. Do they bear dissention? Strife? Share with one another, and the Holy Spirit will guide.

You are all called to be children of the Resurrection. You attain this through your baptism and your active participation in the Perpetual Sacrifice of the Mass. There are so many who disbelieve, so many who attempt to destroy and stop. Their signs are many. The attacks from outside the Church are overt and obvious. But those from within are so subtle—so much good truth surrounding deep and buried falsehood.

The crucifix, the symbol of my most beautiful Son's suffering, is a sign of the perpetuity of His Sacrifice, offered at all times around the world in the Holy Mass. Look to that crucifix, my children. Be the champions of the crucifix of my Son's suffering. To those who have lost faith, the crucifix is a stumbling block, something they want to turn away from, something they want to bury in the past. Their error is so grievous, my children.

Have confidence in my Son's love for His Church and for all His children. His will be done, I assure you. Hold steadfast. Continue in your prayers. Pray for those souls who are lost

---

[26] Our Blessed Mother is referring to the three-week period in which she did not speak to their cenacle.

and wandering, and for those souls charged with their protection who have become complacent.

I love you all, and I leave you with my peace.

MESSAGE FROM MARY
AUGUST 4, 1993

Beautiful children of God, it is I, your Mother, who speaks with you now. I love you all, and I bring you my Son's love. We are joyful in your obedience and your trust.

Great storms are building, my children. You see them as surely as you see the sunrise. This wisdom comes not from yourselves but as a gift from the Father. Speak the truth boldly. Defend your faith. Do this with discretion. Trust your conscience to guide you in these matters, and always rest assured that I am near. For my help, all you need do is open your hearts in prayer.

A great turning point in the fate of your nation and its faith in God will soon be upon you, and I ask you all to pray and offer your sufferings in this cause.

In your personal lives, my children, you must pray for those that will not; you must love for those that cannot; you must have hope for those that will not. I have told you many times to mortify[27] yourselves, to offer these as gifts to the Father; and I ask you to continue in this manner. But look to the little ones [small mortifications]: holding the tongue when you desire to chastise, small little favors, the sufferings of unjust comments or behavior, giving up a desirable morsel of food, or helping a poor person. These are the little flowers that fill the garden. The beautiful rose bushes full of thorns are supplied well enough by God, my children. Concern yourself with the little flowers, those that collect all the dew and absorb the rain and the sun.

---

[27] **Mortify:** to practice ascetic self-discipline; to die to self

I love you all, and I leave you with my Maternal blessing and offer of support. Good-bye, my children.

MESSAGE FROM MARY
AUGUST 18, 1993

Oh, My children, it is I, your Mother, who speaks with you this day. Rest in my arms. Repose your souls and listen to me.

I wish to thank you for all your prayers in support of the Holy Father,[28] the man who truly represents my Son on earth. He suffers so for you, my children. Please continue your prayers for him and for all the Church.

"My children". . . I call you this because it was God's great plan that you be given to me—your hearts and your souls—in a holy adoption. My beautiful Son, Whose words speak through the centuries, gave you to me from the Cross, and in this way, His will will be fulfilled in all of His children through my heart.

What does this mean? When you were little, you looked to your Mother for all your needs: your clothing, your shelter and safety, the very food you ate. She cleaned your soiled bodies. She protected you. This is what I offer your souls, my children, to protect them, to develop them, and to feed them with my maternal care. Many of my children, they fight, they kick and fuss; but I remain always the patient Mother.

I love you all so much and wish you all to abandon yourselves to my will. All your prayers, all your needs, I bring to my most Holy Son, Who looks upon them as the sweet incense they are. Why? Because He knows they belong to the children of His Mother.

I love you all, and I leave you in peace and with my Son's blessings.

---

28 Pope John Paul II

MESSAGE FROM MARY
AUGUST 25, 1993

Beloved children of God, it is I, your Mother, who speaks with you this day. I implore you to come to me. Come to me and bathe in the joy and graces of my Immaculate Heart. I hold you all so dear.

This is a time of preparation, my children. This is a time for you to receive the light, the light that will shine through you to all the world. Avoid dissention and discord. These lead nowhere but to trial. It is this light, which I am preparing you to receive, that will be used so effectively on my Son's behalf for a troubled and dangerous world.

Words without the light have no meaning. A blind man does not see fruit by hearing its description, but the light shining through you onto his soul will increase his vision, his ability to see, and the object of his desire will become readily apparent. You, children, are being prepared as vessels of the light.

Concern yourselves with personal purity of heart, with love, with obedience, with learning and sharing your faith amongst one another. Continue your prayers. I implore you, continue to consecrate yourselves to me from the heart. It is not through words, it is not through prayers—that is, the words used in those prayers—that I prepare you, but in the openness of your hearts, your willingness to respond to my call, your freely giving of yourself to me for the greater glory of my Son.

All glory and honor to God! Praise be to the Father! Praise be to the Son! Praise be to the Holy Spirit!

I love you all, and I leave you now with my peace. Good-bye, my children.

MESSAGE FROM MARY
SEPTEMBER 1, 1993

Oh, my beautiful children, it is I, your Mother, who speaks with you this day. How happy I am, so full of joy at your presence. Surround me with your hearts, my children. Let my love flow into them, for I touch them in a very special way this day. Have hope and trust in me.

At this time, the enemy, who is so strong in these days, increases his attacks on the most Holy Church, from within and without. He attempts to surround and suffocate with falsehood, with accusation, with anger, with blasphemy. Stay constant, my children. Support each other. Pray. Pray often. Always for humility you must ask.

Great things are on the horizon, my children . . . things such as few have ever seen. I am preparing you for this. Do not engage in strife. Do not fight the enemy on his battlefield, for the one he has chosen will lead you to anger and frustration. This tears away at your store of love and hope and faith: the three virtues that you will need so desperately to stay with my Church and with me through its passion.

Share the truth with your light, with your witness, with the evidence of your lives. Never shirk from this duty. God will present you with many great opportunities, and there will be many tests along the way. Hold fast. Cling to the rock of the Church. Absorb its truths with tenderness of heart that I bequeath you, if you respond to my call.

Thank you so much for your beautiful Rosary, filled with such love and tenderness. I love you all, my children. I love you.

MESSAGE FROM JESUS

My children, the strength of your ardor, the love and commitment you show My Mother, is most gratifying to Me. There is nothing you can do that will align you more to My Father's will than to continue in this manner. Rely on her strength. Rely on the power of her prayer. She loves each of you so much. The time is coming when much will be asked of you. But I promise this: a hundred-fold will be returned . . . a thousand-fold. Always keep in mind your heavenly homeland, for I truly long for the day that we will share the great bliss together.

I leave you now, My children, and I ask that you listen to My Mother's words and pray. Together We are arm in arm. We love you all and offer you our support and our strength.

May God bless you all in My Name, in the Name of the Holy Father, and the Most Holy Spirit. Good-bye.

MESSAGE FROM MARY
SEPTEMBER 8, 1993

My beautiful children, it is I, your Mother, who speaks with you this day. I thank you so much for all your gifts, your sacrifices, and your love.

Today is the day that the Holy Church observes my birthday, the birth that heralded man's redemption. It is true that I heralded his redemption, and that I will also herald his judgment—the time of the glorious return of my Son, the time when each will go to his own place. Until that time, my children, there is much to do. My birth was in the glorious pain of my mother, the pain that heralded redemption. Likewise, there will be pain that heralds the coming of my Son. It is so important, my children, that you be prepared. Open your hearts to me. Let me prepare you for the end, when all my children will be with me.

I love you all so much. Remember my words. Practice the virtues. Put forth the effort. Pray for my Son to send His graces to you, to fill you abundantly. In this way, you will grow in perfection. I want you all to be effective witnesses to the world, to all those souls who rest on the edge of a precipice. You will not convince them by words or doctrine, but by the way you lead your lives. This you know, my children. You feel this in your hearts. I've told you so, so many times.

Rest in me throughout the day. Perform all your acts of kindness and love in virtue, in my name, and I promise to lead you to my Son . . . the most glorious resting place. I love you all, my children, and I thank you so much for your prayers, your devotions, and your dutiful love.

Good-bye.

MESSAGE FROM MARY
SEPTEMBER 15, 1993

My beautiful children, it is I, your Mother, who speaks with you now. I love you all so much, and I am so happy that you gather in this small cenacle, my little cenacle of children, small and hidden from the world. One day you will shower them with graces—those who do not see now, those who do not feel now, those who do not love now.

I am sorrowful[29] because they would kill the Love, and because they hate the Love. Stay in your prayer, my children. The enemy is near. His name is Division, and his ill winds blow across you and across the Church. Let me prepare you, let me mold you, fill you with my love and the graces that flow so abundantly from my Son. I am constantly with you to support you, to help you, lest you fall.

In the proper time, in the proper place, many you meet will look at you in a different way. Their eyes will be opened, and they will see. How will you appear to them? What will they see? This, my children, is why I prepare you. This is why you must take the time necessary to develop, to grow, so that you may spring forth as the beautiful flowers of the Lord.

I love you all, and I leave you with my kisses and blessings. Good-bye, my children.

---

[29] This day was the feast day of Our Lady of Sorrows.

MESSAGE FROM MARY
SEPTEMBER 22, 1993

Beautiful children of God, it is I, your Mother, who speaks with you now. I thank you for your beautiful Rosary, your prayers of consolation for my Sorrowful Heart.

So many pull away. So many hide from the truth. At times we feel overwhelmed and distressed, without power or authority to affect so much good that is necessary. I know you fear redemption for many. Redemption is in jeopardy for so many of my children. And that is why I come, in this way, to so many of my children around the world—to confound falsehood, to promote truth, to bring my Son's sheep back to Him.

You will be employed as lights, my children, in the proper time. Do not feel distress at those who do not see or do not understand. I assure you they will be touched, and only the most obstinate will remain separated from us.

Continue to pray. Continue to allow me to mold you, to perfect you. Forgive yourselves. Forgive your pasts. Rejoice in God's presence at all times. Know that I am with you and that I support you. I truly say that this is the time of my Son's mercy. This is the time when His holiness and magnificence will be made manifest throughout the world. Rejoice, my children, and prepare.

I love you all, and I leave you with my Son's peace . . . and my abundant graces and blessings, as bestowed on me from the Father.

I love you all. Good-bye.

MESSAGE FROM MARY
SEPTEMBER 29, 1993

My beautiful children, it is I, your Mother, who speaks with you this day. I bring you the joy and consolation of my Victorious and Immaculate Heart. Be at peace, my children. I *implore* you to do what I ask of you: pray, fast, do penance, think of God and all His beauty, avoid discord and dissention.

My Son sends you many gifts of consolation, many souls for you to touch. A test for you, my children: if you feel dissention, strife, anguish in your discussions and contact, those souls were not sent by my Son. Do not react. Do not behave in this way, for their souls may be touched in a different way at a different time. These souls are not for you, my children.

I ask you to unite your contrite hearts with my Immaculate Heart, the heart pierced with the sword, and to offer them at every Mass you attend. In this way, we are united in our small and humble ways to the Sacred Heart of my Son, that was offered to the Father for all mankind. In this way, we participate in the Perpetual Sacrifice, in the perpetual redemption of man.

My children, I pray for you daily that you do not lose your faith, a gift bestowed on you from the Father, Himself— a gift that allows you to see what others cannot, to hear what others cannot, and to feel what others cannot. I *implore* you to maintain your daily Rosaries, your renunciation of so many worldly pleasures, your patience and faith and perseverance. This faith you will need. It will become so important to you as we approach the "end of ends," the "time of times," that period for which I have been preparing you.

I love you all, my children, and I leave you now with my blessings . . . and a kiss. Good-bye, my children.

MESSAGE FROM MARY
OCTOBER 6, 1993

Beautiful children of God, it is I, your Mother, who speaks with you this day. I bring you my love and my special blessing, a maternal blessing for my children who must live in the world. Cast aside your fears, your anxieties. Live in my Immaculate Heart, the heart that loves you so.

There is so much I wish to share with you, my children, so much I wish to give you. In due time, all will become so clear to you, all will be understood. For now, I ask you to persevere in your prayers, in your support for each other.

My children, a time of darkness approaches. You have been given the grace to see this. You see through the mists and confusion that the enemy puts forth. What he detests most, what he fears most, is your gentleness, your humility, your love. He can test you; he may try you; but stay close to my heart, my children, and I promise you protection. I say again, cast aside all fear. Do not speculate about the future. Today's worries are enough. Love one another. Be at peace.

I offer you a special blessing this day, one that will fill your hearts with joy, love, and an appreciation for my Son, for He is the "End" I prepare you for. He is the "All" that will fulfill you.

I leave you, my children, with my love and a very special blessing. Good-bye.

MESSAGE FROM JESUS

My children, My brothers and sisters, it is I, your saving Lord, Who speaks with you now. I thank you for your service and the offering of your prayers. I come to you this day at My Mother's request to let you know the special place I hold for all of you. Those who My Mother blesses are very special to Me and most dear to Me.

At times your crosses feel heavy. The evil one shakes them and bounces on them. He distresses you. He whips up confusion and tempts you. Hold fast, My children. The special blessing My Mother has given you this day is a blessing of peace and strength. Call upon her often. Truly consecrate yourself to her Immaculate Heart for My Mother is the Jewel of the Universe and the Joy of Joys.

I leave you now, My children. Good-bye.

MESSAGE FROM MARY
OCTOBER 8, 1993

My beautiful children, it is I, your Mother, who is with you this evening. It fills my heart with such joy to see my children happily sharing. I love you all so much, and I assure you I am with you always—at no time closer than I am with you this evening.

My children, it is good that you share the messages I bring to you. We have passed the anniversary[30] of the first time I came to you in this way, and my purpose is to prepare you, to prepare you to play your roles in the glorious victory of my Immaculate Heart. My words to you illuminate the Gospel and bring you closer to my Son. In this way, He is glorified to the Father, and heaven sings in harmony to the joys of your salvation and of the salvation of those whom you will touch.

This evening I will come to you in a special way. All those who feel the call in their hearts I will speak to this evening.[31] Be not afraid. Put aside your fears. Open your hearts to me.

I love you all, my children, and I leave you now with my peace. Good-bye.

---

[30] Our Lady first spoke to the cenacle on October 7th, 1992, the feast of Our Lady of the Rosary.

[31] This refers to each member who wanted to pray with a couple of the group members. Through Walter, they also received a personal message from Our Blessed Mother.

MESSAGE FROM MARY
OCTOBER 13, 1993

My beloved children, it is I, your Mother, who speaks with you this day. I love you all so dearly, and I thank you for your prayers and sacrifices and your small sufferings to be with me this day. This is the anniversary of the day I came at the beginning of your century to warn and prepare the world for God's mercy and His justice.[32]

I implore those children of mine, who out of fear or pride, arrogance, or lack of faith, attempt to make religion conform to the world. Please hear my call and repent. Those of my children who give in to lusts of the body and lead others to do so for justification of their own actions, I implore to hear my call and repent For those who blame others for their misfortune, and in turn, turn that blame to anger and hatred, I ask them to hear my call and repent.

You, my children, are the light of the world. You have been and are being prepared to go out and witness to all my children, to bring them back to the fold before it is too late, for time is so very short, my children. You have no strength of yourselves. All this comes from graces. That is why it is so important that you pray and fast and receive the Sacraments, for it is at these times that the Holy Spirit truly dwells within you. Practice virtue. Perform works of mercy. In this way, you spread the message of the Good News, the Good News that is ignored by so many.

Oh, my children, so many of your brothers and sisters—dear loved ones, beautiful souls—focus so much of their

---

[32] Our Blessed Mother appeared in Fatima, Portugal, on October 13, 1917, where 70,000 people collectively witnessed the miracle of the sun.

energies on the world and its bitter fruits. Pray for them, my children. Unite your prayers to mine.

I leave you now with my peace and the abundant graces that flow to you from meeting with me in this way.

Good-bye, my children.

MESSAGE FROM MARY
OCTOBER 20, 1993

My beautiful children, it is I, your Mother, who speaks with you this day. I bring you comfort and joy, and the graces from my beautiful Son, Who loves you so.

Continue your prayers, my children. Pray fervently for the reparation of the world's sins, for the holy wounds that were inflicted upon my Son. My Son's hands, that performed so many beautiful and wondrous works, were pinned to the wood to stop them. His lovely feet, that traversed so many miles spreading the Good News, were brutally spiked. They crowned His head with vicious thorns, as if to imprison His holy doctrine. And finally, they pierced the heart that offered hope and salvation to all the world. He was then held up as a sign of His destruction, as an image of the enemy's victory. But instead, that Cross became the symbol of the intersection of two destinies: the destiny of heaven and of earth in a new creation, a new and glorious creation for which you are all being prepared.

So continue your prayers of reparation for all those souls who do not see salvation. I love you, my children, and I leave you now with my peace, my love, and my praise for your perseverance.

Good-bye, my children.

MESSAGE FROM JESUS
OCTOBER 27, 1993

Children of God, peace be with you. I love you all so much and am so happy with your prayers and all your efforts on behalf of My Church.

I come to you this day to speak of My Mother, the woman who said "yes," and the Mother of you all. She succeeded in a world full of sin and temptation, where Eve had failed. She accomplished all this with an abundance of trust and hope, lacking many of the gifts with which Eve was endowed. She was a perfect mirror that reflected My hope and My sorrows, My joys, My successes and failures in life. And now, in all My glory, she remains that perfect mirror. My light, My love, My joy flows to you, My children . . . through her.

And there is no better emissary for My kingdom than My holy Mother. She is here to bring so many of My brothers and sisters, My children, back to the Church. And she will be successful, and she will complete her mission in time. And I ask all of you to help—to reflect in your own lives, in your own ways, My hope and My mercy—for it is true that time is short.

I love you, My children, and I leave you with My blessing and love.

MESSAGE FROM MARY
NOVEMBER 3, 1993

My beloved children, it is I, your Mother, who speaks with you this day. Your hearts are so full of love and joy and peace. You are truly my family, my beautiful ones. You bring joy to my heart. I long for the day when I can gather you in my arms.

Be not afraid. Fear not injustice, desperation, pain, for I am your Mother, and a good mother provides for her children. This is not to say you will be relieved of trials and burdens, for it is in this way you will achieve true freedom. Rather, I promise you the graces to embrace your crosses, to join with me in humble adoration of the Blessed Trinity.

My heart is so sorrowful, my children, for those sons and daughters of mine who daily blaspheme the Lord, Our God, and their very natures. My heart is pierced with the many swords of those children of mine who offer their brothers and sisters only injustice, starvation, hatred—the devil's vices. Soon it will seem as if the love has gone cold. But it will not, my children. They will bury it under all their ingratitude, their service of the enemy, their filth, their rejection of the Father's will for them. The enemy knows this, and he continues to pile on layer after layer. But he also knows that the fire smolders, and it will consume it all in a glorious flame, a flame that will sear all men's souls: the glorious love of our Almighty Lord and Creator.

I love you all so much, my children, and I offer you the graces to endure with patience, with love, and with submissive childlike understanding of the Father's will.

Good-bye, my children.

MESSAGE FROM MARY
NOVEMBER 10, 1993

My beautiful children, it is I, your Mother, who speaks with you this day. I offer you my prayers, my consolation, and my abundant love, the love which is a gift from the Father and comes to you through the Cross of my Son.

The Cross is truly a sign of contradiction to the world and what it finds important. They stumble over it. They fall headlong over it, without understanding or concern. What was started at the Annunciation, culminated in the Cross, the glorious death of my Son, which brought new life to all the world. Keep the Cross always in your hearts, my children. Bear it well in this life. For as clay is molded by the Father into human beings—in life, so are your souls.

My children, I come to you in this way to prepare you to understand and carry your crosses—first, with resignation . . . eventually, with joy—because it is through that burden, through the hard work of the soul, that you are united with the Father and with the Son and with the Most Holy Spirit, Who fills you to completeness. I know crosses appear fearful. They are so heavy. Sometimes we complain about the size or their shape. But they do not matter. Do not compare them, do not reject them. Go to my Son for the needed graces, for the strength to endure. He is always there, and He will never leave His sheep to the wolves.

I love you, my children, and I leave you now with my peace, my love, and my blessing, which comes to you from the Blessed Trinity. Good-bye, my children.

MESSAGE FROM MARY
NOVEMBER 17, 1993

My children, it is I, your Mother, who is with you this day, and I thank you for your prayers and your beautiful flowery gifts.[33] They please my heart so. I implore you to continue to gather with me in this way. This is our little cenacle, my children. Here we commune. Here I bring you joyous words to fill your hearts, to protect you from the great time of trial.

The time is approaching soon. . . . it gathers strength . . . the great trial of unbelief. That is why I come to you in this way, and that is why I offer you my protection, for the world will challenge you. Even those children consecrated to me at birth will devour the souls of their brothers and sisters.

Children, my Son offers you the Tree of Life, the tree from which humanity was banished so long ago—the tree, the access to which my Son earned for you in His glorious Sacrifice. The fruit of this tree, my children, is His body. Adore it as it lays in my arms, pulled from the cross of pain. This is why, my children, I wish all of you to think of me as the Mother of the Holy Eucharist.

Go to Adoration, attend Mass often, spend that time that your duties allow, for this is the food of souls. This is where your protection lies. In the Eucharist, my Son resides as surely as He remained God in my arms. And as you adore Him in the Eucharist, know that you adore Him in my arms. So many of my children reject or deny the fruit of this tree, and what saddens me more, they even reject the tree from which it comes. That is why all your prayers are so important, my

---

[33] It seems that our Blessed Mother is referring to the flowers some members brought this day and placed at the feet of the statue of Our Lady.

children, to soften their hearts. Pray to soften their hearts. I will protect you.

I am your Mother, and those that consecrate themselves to me will not be lost. I leave you now, my children. Ponder my words.

I love you. Good-bye.

MESSAGE FROM MARY
NOVEMBER 19, 1993

My beautiful children, it is I, your Mother, who is with you this evening, this joyous evening of sharing, seeing all my beautiful children together, happily in conversation, purified by the spirit of love, in joy of true companionship. Meeting in this way is an important part of your preparation, my children. You practice virtue; you learn to understand one another; you strengthen one another; and you learn to live the way of the cross, the joyous and happy way of the cross, the cross which strengthens you because of its burden.

Soon begins the joyous time of Advent. The birth of your Redeemer looms close on the horizon . . . the focal point of history . . . the love of all the universe. Think of that beautiful child, containing all creation—that creation that was born at the sound of His voice and that lives in His Word.

Quiet all your souls. Be at peace. Always show a peaceful demeanor. Prepare yourselves constantly for stillness. In this way, I touch each of your hearts. I truly come to you in a special way, and I envelope you in my maternal protection. Fear nothing. Hope for everything. Praise my Son, praise His Father, praise the Spirit between Them.

I love you, my children, and I leave you with my peace and my abundant blessings that come to you directly from the Son.

Good-bye, my children.

MESSAGE FROM MARY
NOVEMBER 24, 1993

My beautiful children, it is I, your Mother, who is with you this day, a day in which you prepare for your feast of Thanksgiving. What a beautiful grace it is that allows you to participate with your loved ones in such a day. Make it a day of joy, a day of comfort, a day of sharing, and a day of remembrance for those less fortunate. I *implore* you to make it a day of prayer. Think of God's graces and His immense love for you.

I pray with all my heart, my most Sorrowful and Immaculate Heart, that those hardened and stony hearts of my wayward children will allow me to soften them with my maternal blessings. This is why your prayers are so important to me, my children. Your gathering in this way has more power than you can imagine. Oh, if only they would follow God's law instead of their own. They are like a sick child who rejects the food that is good for them and will bring them to health.

I love you all so, my children. I am so thankful for the time you give me. Your prayers are a great consolation for my pierced and sorrowful heart. Please be at peace. Retain your vigilance. Pray always for the grace of endurance, for this is the grace that you will need most—for you truly will live a life of beauty and a life of trial, and in this way gain salvation for yourselves and so many more.

Good-bye, my children.

MESSAGE FROM MARY
DECEMBER 1, 1993

Beautiful and glorious children of God, I love you so. This is your Mother, who speaks with you this day, the Mother who loves you, the Mother who brings you heavenly consolation and the graces of my beautiful Son.

Many changes are afoot. Many dark trials for the Church, for those who believe. These times have been prophesied. Do not be concerned or afraid, because I protect you, and I prepare you. Let holiness be your goal. Have faith and confidence, because the Spirit is with you all. And though this is Satan's hour, I have come to crush his head, to root out evil and to unite the Father's children. I accomplish this by preparing the way for my glorious Son. This is by right of the singular grace freely given to me from God the Father, God the Son, and God the Holy Spirit—one God united in will, united in love for all humanity, the God Who graced me Queen of Heaven and strengthens me for my task.

This is a great contest for souls, my children, a great battle—a battle in which my greatest weapon will be your humility, your holiness, and your perseverance. You attain these through cooperation with freely given graces: by prayer; by mortification; by fasting; by receipt of the Sacraments, and by uniting yourself with my holy task, through your consecrations. Mortifications . . . fasting, my children, is so important. Prayer trains the soul, but fasting . . . mortifications, train the will. It is through the will that the enemy can attack you. The stronger your will, the stronger your ability to resist him. Remember this, my children.

I love you all, and I give you my Motherly promise to never abandon you, to never leave your side. All you need do in great trials of temptation or depression is reach for me.

Reach out, my children. I love you all, and I leave you with a Mother's love and my blessing for you all. Good-bye.

MESSAGE FROM MARY
DECEMBER 8, 1993

Beautiful children of God, My children, it is I, your Mother, who speaks with you this most beautiful day, the day when our Church celebrates the dawn of the new creation.[34] My children, I thank you for all your prayers, your supplications, and I thank you for your consecrations[35] and devotions. All of these I hold most tenderly to my heart. They are a beautiful gift, a gift meant for the salvation of so many. And I thank you all for honoring my request.[36]

My beautiful children, what glorious gifts God has bestowed on us. He has shown us the way, the path to light and to holiness. He offers Himself so that we may cling to His abundant strength and mercy, find sustenance in His love, and enjoy His presence. Striving for holiness is so important, my children, because in the purity of holiness, the Holy Spirit resides, unhampered by dirt and filth, by the complications and scorn of the world. My children, my love, truly I tell you, the Father's love is beyond boundaries, beyond time and distance, and the closer you come to Him, the closer you will come to that reality.

Long ago, Satan, the evil one, the deceiver, introduced sin in the world. He did this by guile. He did this by seduction. He seduced the woman unblemished.[37] In

---

[34] Feast of the Immaculate Conception

[35] Many members completed the 33 day St. Louis de Montfort consecration "to Jesus through Mary" today in front of the Blessed Sacrament, prior to the start of the cenacle.

[36] It is said that Our Blessed Mother appeared to a nun named Sister Pierina of Italy in 1946 to request an hour of grace at noon on Dec. 8. She requested the recitation of the 51st Psalm and one hour of uninterrupted prayer. We assumed that Mary was thanking us for our response to this particular request.

[37] Eve

response to this, the Father's plan was made manifest in time—not by seduction, not by guile—but by openness, by love, and request. Oh, how I have been blessed, His lowly handmaid! He truly exalts the lowly and humbles the proud.

Thank you, my children, so much for coming to me this day in such a beautiful way. And I leave you with my peace and the abundant blessings of the Almighty Father, the Son, and the Holy Spirit. Good-bye, my children.

MESSAGE FROM MARY TO LYDIA[38]
DECEMBER 15, 1993

Beautiful daughter, it is I, your Mother, who speaks with you this day, in the presence of loving witnesses.[39] Oh, the joy and sorrow you bring to my heart, my child—the joy of your sacrifice, the sorrow of your suffering. What a great gift you are to my Son and to all those souls whom you bless.

In a little while, at the proper time, I will come for you and bring you directly to my Son, Who will be your complete joy, and you will see Him and love Him forever. This I promise you, my child. Persevere. Remain strong. The demons, they torture you as they tortured my Son. Your respite is my Son. Your joy is my Son. Your cross is heavy, my child, and it brings me to tears; but your strength, your power resides in my Son. I know this because I see my Son in you. I cry tears for your pain, and through these tears, so many will be saved. Because of your faith, there will be so much healing. Your children, dear little one, are mine. You have consecrated them to me, and so they shall remain.

Your greatest work is about to begin. In joy, you will be with me. Your great work will be the salvation of so many, the help of so many. I know, my child, that at this time, your consolation is a bitter fire on your tongue.[40] But it will seem so little to the great joy you will experience. The cross must be carried a little longer, my child. This is because of your great strength, the great strength you have because its source is my Son to Whom you've totally devoted yourself.

---

[38] Lydia: A member of our cenacle prayer group who joyfully and courageously endured great and prolonged sufferings from cancer

[39] Our Blessed Mother could be referring to the members of our cenacle who knelt around Lydia's bed to pray the Rosary, and/or to other heavenly witnesses who may have been present.

[40] Lydia was without consolation, enduring intense suffering without reprieve.

Fear not for your children, for they are filled with abundant blessings. There are so many little ones, so many of my lost children that have no mother they recognize. I pray that God will open their hearts to see me.

I love you so, my dear Lydia. Know that I am always with you. Call on me . . . call on me in times of desperate need, and I will come to you. I will console your heart and prepare you for my Son.

Good-bye, my beautiful daughter. Good-bye.

MESSAGE FROM MARY
DECEMBER 22, 1993

My beautiful children, it is I, your Mother, who speaks with you this day. What a beautiful day! What joy my heart is filled with to see you and your families prepare for the glorious feast, the feast that commemorates the birth of our God.

What a divine mystery this is that the God, in Whose image we were created, descended upon us in His perfect love and in His perfect justice. For only perfect justice compels all of us to receive my Son in our hearts and in our lives, and in particular, through the Blessed and Holy Eucharist. It allows us to be one with Him and allows you to have all your sins, all the scrapes and burns and sorrows of life, to be absorbed into His suffering . . . His suffering on the Cross, which is the perfection of both love and justice.

The Father loves you so. Like little children, you try to walk, and He helps you. His gentle and loving hand caresses you and rewards you for your efforts. At times, at your weakest points, He does carry you; but it's the effort that brings Him joy, and it is through this great and glorious effort, that comes to you only through the grace of my glorious Son, that you will learn to walk in the light. And this light will be a witness to all my children. Oh, if only they would all accept instead of reject this light. And that is why we continue to pray. That is why I continue to intercede, on behalf of all of them, to the Father.

Continue your prayers, my children. Continue your struggles because I promise you the abundant joys of my Son. Allow all your suffering, your joys, your trials and successes, to be absorbed in the Eucharist and become one with His Sacrifice on the Cross.

I love you all, my children, and I leave you with my blessing.

Good-bye.

MESSAGE FROM MARY
DECEMBER 29, 1993

Beautiful children, it is I, your Mother, who speaks with you this day . . . and I wish to speak about the love of my beautiful Child, the Infant I hold so tenderly in my arms, the Infant Whose love is the joy and the light of the world, for without Him there is no light, and there is no love.

The same rage and hatred that compelled a man to murder "the innocents"[41] at the threat of my Son, also compels a dreaded attack upon your faith and our Church. It is an attack based on greed and covetousness for the goods of this world, without concern for the fate of souls. This hatred and greed, which is spawned from the enemy's curse, is cured only by prayer . . . prayer and sacrifice . . . and the love and acceptance of my Son. Accept Him into your hearts. Let Him fill you.

To offer yourself in words is good; but to offer yourself in deeds is far greater. I promise you great joy in this offering because He accepts all who come to Him in humility and perseverance. Please meditate upon His beauty and His wonderful acceptance of the world, that He lay so innocent and trusting in my motherly arms. He is our Creator, our God, our Beginning, and our End. Love Him. Love Him with everything you have.

Good-bye, my children. I leave you with my peace and abundant graces and blessings.

---

41 This surely refers to the children slaughtered at the order of King Herod in Bethlehem, following the birth of Jesus. (Matthew 2:16-18)

MESSAGE FROM MARY
JANUARY 12, 1994

My beautiful children, it is I, your Mother, the Mother of your Lord, who speaks with you this day. I thank and bless you all for your prayers, your mortifications and sacrifices, that you offer in my name. They bring abundant joy to heaven.

My children, through perseverance, you will achieve the joys and happiness that are promised to you—such joy and happiness as is impossible for the human mind to conceive, everlasting and without limit. So many of my children jeopardize this great gift. They do not realize or see the precipice over which they hover.

Oh, my children, even the elect could be fooled, if it were possible. The why of Satan's strength and power is part of the mystery of salvation. It is enough for you to know this truth, and to pray for your brothers and sisters who are blind, who fall prey to their desires—desires that are promulgated by science, and with that same science, apparently justified by consensus. There is nothing new in these desires, my children. They spring from the concupiscence[42] that is as old as "the fall." So many of my children become trapped. They feel that by this "consensus," God's will is done. But the reality is that they only throw off their crosses, and in their guilt, attempt to remove all crosses, even from the most obstinate and obvious of faults.

My children, predilection to sin, suffering by temptation, is more real than physical torture or starvation. It is from this that so many of my children suffer. I cry for them. But my Son gathers my tears, and the day will come, my children, the day

---

[42] **Concupiscence:** strong desire; to desire ardently; inclination to sin

promised, when bright and glorious will my Son wash away these evils from your land with my tears. This is what you prepare for, my children. This is why I come to you. Watch and pray with me. I love you all, and I leave you now with my praise and glory and honor.

MESSAGE FROM MARY
JANUARY 19, 1994

Beautiful children of God, it is I, your Mother, who speaks with you this day. I offer you my love and many consolations to strengthen you during this time of trial. For some of you, this trial is small, barely noticeable. For others it is a great weight. Such is the ebb and flow of life.

I assure you, my children, all that are consecrated to me, all my beautiful children, are led by my tender touch. In times of decision, search your hearts, pray for forgiveness and the guidance of the Holy Spirit. Know that firmness in defense of the truth is always an act of charity. False argumentation, deceit, judgmentalism, are all weapons of Satan, and it is these he uses as wedges to drive you apart. Stay close to me, my children. Remain in my tender embrace.

Know that I am always with you through all the stumbles, all the small failures that you feel are so great. Know that my love is firm and stands forever . . . this love which is the gift and grace of my Son, my Creator and the Source of all love. Always go forth as lights, my children. Offer up these crosses, these anxieties, pains and concerns, as great pearls, beautiful jewels, the true flowers of the universe that please the Father so.

Thank you, my children, for being obedient, for holding back from that closeness you desire. When the time is right, you may approach. Know that this obedience is a great badge of merit to which the heavens sing praise.

Good-bye, my children. I love you all, and leave you with the blessings of The Most High, through my Son, my Lord Jesus. All glory and honor to Him forever! Amen.

MESSAGE FROM MARY
JANUARY 26, 1994

My beautiful children, it is I, your Mother, who speaks with you this day. I love you all so much, and I ask you to remember always that I am near you. I constantly plead for you to my Son that you may stay on His path and endure to the end. This is always in my prayers.

This week you have been granted a glorious gift.[43] The blessing of this great and glorious gift will manifest itself in time. You will see its work in many ways. I tell you this gift is the victory of my Immaculate Heart. The ground is swelling with those who have consecrated themselves to me and do my bidding. It is a gentle and humble victory, a victory of love and a victory of hearts.

All over the world, beautiful oases[44] of my Son's love are being born anew. These oases offer refuge and security from the works and pomps of the enemy. To be a part of this, my children, is a great blessing. Know that you have been loved from the beginning. My victory will be sweet and necessary, as we enter into the period of purification for the world. Know this, my children, and be glad.

I love you all, and I leave you with my peace and blessings. Continue steadfast in your prayers. Pray from your hearts, my children. Good-bye.

---

[43] It seems likely that Mary is referring to their bishop who was being installed that week.
[44] May be a reference to cenacles of prayer

MESSAGE FROM MARY
FEBRUARY 2, 1994

My beautiful children, it is I, your Mother, who speaks with you this day, and I thank you so much for your beautiful Rosary. Your prayers of reflection, your feelings of joy and remorse, are pleasing to my Son.

Only through my Son can redemption be found. He entered His Father's presence in humble fashion, mortified by poverty and the love of the simple. The Father's presence cannot be won by pride or arrogance or force of will. It cannot be earned or purchased. Only by submission, gentle and loving submission to my Son and His Church, is that door opened.

My children, there are so many opportunities for grace, offered to you by the Church. The Sacraments are truly grace-filled gifts from my Son to all of you. *Go to them as often as you can.* Inspire others by your faith to do likewise, for there, is true salvation for yourselves, for those whom you pray, and indeed for the whole world.

Be humble. Be charitable. Always question your motives, for all my children are imperfect. Pray always that God's will be done. Have confidence in me as your Mother, that I will guide you through all the difficult challenges of life— for those of you who consecrate yourselves to me I will never abandon.

I love you all so much. Please know that I pray for you constantly. I petition my Son always on your behalf. Know that I am always near you.

Good-bye, my children.

MESSAGE FROM MARY
FEBRUARY 9, 1994

Beautiful children of God, it is I, your Mother, who speaks with you this day. I thank you for your beautiful prayers, for they console my sorrowful heart. I use them for best advantage. They precede the way of the Spirit and warm the hearts that are necessary to be warmed.

I urge you, my children, continue in your mortifications. Your small offerings and sacrifice of worldly pleasures, a resistance to desires of the flesh, are so important for your formation. You must know, my children, I desire so much a deepening of your spirituality, and I offer you a closeness that is attained by very few in this world. There is but a small requirement, and that is the recognition that you can only serve one master.

I know it is so difficult for you, my children, for yours is a society of the flesh and it is so very difficult to go without so many small pleasures. But if you do these things, at a time of your choosing, the benefits of grace will truly astound you. Your prayer will deepen, and you will come closer to my precious Son. That is, above all, what I desire most, my children, for it is there that my plan is effected. Why? Because if you are prepared to receive my Son—truly prepared—the light of this preparation will show to all those you influence, all those you know, and all those you will come to know. At the proper time, they will see this light. Many will surprise you with their repentance and a turning towards the Lord.

Be ever vigilant, my children, from those spirits that would attempt to dissuade you, to move you away from me, to move you away from the Church. Please know, my children, that I love you all, and I leave you with my abundant

130

graces and blessings, by the power given to me by the Most Blessed Trinity. Good-bye, my children.

MESSAGE FROM MARY
FEBRUARY 23, 1994

My beautiful children, it is I, your Mother, who speaks with you this day. Rest yourselves, my children. Quiet your hearts. Listen to my words, for they are words of Maternal wisdom.

My Lord and Creator, my Blessed Son, has consented to allow me to speak with you in this way, for a small time. But it is a precious time because you are being prepared for the destiny of your souls, the destiny of eternal bliss in the arms of the Word made flesh. In Him is all love, all mercy, all justice. He is supreme, my children. He is your Creator made sensible so that you may know, love, and obey.

I love you all so much, my children, and it is so important that you come to know my Son's love. Understand its purpose because it is life giving. From His love springs all that is . . . and all that will be.

During this time, my children, fast, do penance, pray for the forgiveness of sins. This is so important because the weight of sin grows so heavy. God, Who is merciful, must be just, my children. So again, I ask you to pray and fast, do penance., unite with my Sorrowful Heart.

My children, my dear children, I implore you to stay with me during this time of trial. Comfort me in my affliction. It gladdens me that you will never know my sorrow, and I hold for each of you the certainty of incredible joy that will be yours, if you persevere.

Good-bye, my children.

MESSAGE FROM MARY
MARCH 2, 1994

My children, it is I, your Mother, who speaks with you now—a Mother of joy and sorrows, a Mother who will lead you through the darkness. The Vicar of my Son[45] steers the boat in which you are all riding out the fierce storms. It rides upon a sea of murky waters, filled with pain, sorrow, hatred, envy—all the poisons of the enemy. The storms blow hard. It makes it very hard for you, my children, to keep your balance. But my Son's Vicar is ever steady at the helm. Rest secure in the knowledge of this.

Know that I come to you, in this way, to comfort and aid, to give you courage, to strengthen you, for it is truly a time of doubt, and a time of suffering and sorrow. I know, my children, you look about you, you see the net that is to be used for the harvest, and it is rent and torn by division, by apostasy, by dissent and hatred. And those that have damaged this net leave for other boats. But I tell you this: a time is coming when you will be ordered to cast the nets, and the harvest will be so great that many of those who left will return to help, for their nets will be empty.[46] The fish will be attracted by the light of my Son's love, which will make the sea clear and beautiful again.

I thank you so much for your prayers, my children. Your most beautiful Rosary was so pleasing to me. Such prayer is so pleasing to my Son. I tell you this day, they ascend to His throne, borne by the angels. Be at peace. Be united. Love and support one another. *Do not gauge events by time.* Rest secure in the knowledge that I am always with you.

---

45 Message given during the pontificate of Pope John Paul II

46 This may refer to the time after The Warning, also called the Illumination of Conscience

Praise be the Father! Praise be the Son, Our Lord Jesus! Praise be Their Most Holy Spirit!

I leave you now my children, and know that I love you always. Good-bye.

MESSAGE FROM MARY
MARCH 9, 1994

My beautiful children, it is I, your Mother, who speaks with you this day. Again I thank you for your prayers and for your special offerings during this Lenten season. They truly warm my heart. Please be attentive to my words this day, my children.

Make a special commitment at this time to attend Mass with special fervor and to put aside your private devotions in my Son's presence. Participate fully in the Mass. Listen and concentrate on the words. Respond from the heart. What a beautiful gift it is for you, my children, to have the Mass said in your language so that you may see and understand and participate in the Church's greatest prayer.

Intentional avoidance of attention slows your progress because it ties you to busyness and to distraction. To attend Mass with a willful desire to allow your mind to disassociate itself from the liturgy is like ascending a mountain with your eyes closed shut. To ascend, you must see to grasp, to hold on . . . and this is so important.

Remain in my heart through your prayers and consecrations to me. I am a sure guide to my Son, Who loves you all so much, and Who desires to spend eternity with you. Let His Spirit rest upon you. Enjoy His pleasing consolation.

I leave you now with my love, my blessing, and my prayers.

Good-bye, my children.

MESSAGE FROM MARY
MARCH 16, 1994

Oh, My beautiful children, it is I, your Mother, who speaks with you this day. I love you all so much and wish to extend to you heaven's deepest gratitude for your beautiful Rosary prayers.

This day I asked my legions to pray with you, my children, to pray for the Church, to pray for all those souls who will be victims of chastisement and suffering. My children, earthquakes, famine, floods, physical tortures of every kind, are not the chastisements to fear, for those that leave the faith will surely ask the hills to fall in on them and the earth to cover them, because they believe this will end their suffering. Oh, my children, that is only the beginning of the most unimaginable sufferings. *Words cannot describe the despair, the pain, the anguish and torment of eternal separation from the Triune God—a separation that will never, never end.* That my children must suffer such defeat sorrows my heart.

The only remedy, my children, for their pride, their rebellion, is prayer. That is why it is so important you remain united. Of course you have your private devotions, your different missions in your daily lives. No . . . I speak of unity in this prayer; I speak of unity of purpose in this gathering, for it is here that I help you to grow. It is here that my Son strengthens you through the power of the Holy Spirit. It is here that you are asked to be Mary at my Son's feet.[47] Leave the works of Martha outside. And furthermore, do not judge the Marys for their lack of support for your work and your labors. Rather, become like the Marys because my Son assures

---

[47] Our Lady is referring to the Gospel story of Martha and Mary, the sisters of Lazarus, found in Luke 10:38-42.

you that this will never be taken from you . . . the eternal bliss of His presence.

I love you all so, my children, and I leave you now with my blessing and a maternal kiss for each of you. Good-bye.

MESSAGE FROM MARY
MARCH 23, 1994

"Beautiful children of God". . . what splendor and glory there is in that name. It fills my heart with such joy to call you this. I am truly your Mother, and the Mother of your Lord.

As the bronze serpent[48] was raised in the desert, so was my Son raised to become "sin" and the salvation for all the world. It is God's promise that all who gaze upon Him in faith shall live with Him forever. What does this mean, my children, to gaze upon Him in faith? I assure you, faith is His gift to you. Your gift to Him is your gaze, your action.

My children, the virtues[49] are great and blessed gifts, graces from the Triune God. Many of these graces are with all my children, no matter how buried, no matter how hidden, especially the grace to desire unity with God. Dear little ones, these gifts are given to you to use. Do not hide them away because like beautiful and gentle flowers, they don't keep unless they are cultivated and worked. They will slowly dissipate and flow to others more worthy. Obedience, forbearance, humility . . . they are so important, my children. Through them faith grows, hope grows, the love of God and your brother grows.

Please heed my words. Know that I love you all so much. How can I love you less, my children? . . . for I freely and without reservation offered my Son to the Father in that horrible holocaust so long ago. Please do not waste this precious gift. Renew yourselves at Easter time. Reach out to those whom you have embittered or chastised unfairly.

---

48 This Old Testament event is found in the book of Numbers 21:4-9.

49 **Virtue:** a habit that perfects the powers of the soul and inclines one to do good. The three highest virtues are the Theological Virtues (Faith, Hope, Charity) which are infused supernatural means whereby the human person's whole ethical, religious, and spiritual life is directed towards the possession of God (Baltimore Catechism).

Accept them into your hearts. Be joyful. Now is a time for recollection.

I leave you with my love and blessings. Good-bye.

MESSAGE FROM MARY
MARCH 30, 1994

My beautiful children, it is I, your Mother, who speaks with you this day. Your Beloved is with me, and I ask you to stay near my heart during these last days of trial.[50]

The darkness and shadows are thickest before the dawn, the dawn that you celebrate in a few short days: the glorious Resurrection of my Son, Our Lord, the Christ. Oh, glory of glories! . . . this greatest day of creation! . . . for on this day, the redemption was complete, love was secured, friendship established. My children, on that day, let your hearts ring with love, like the bell of my Son's churches. Let this love resound throughout the world. You need not express it. It is important that you possess it.

My children, I long for the day when you will be at my side before my Son's throne, enjoying His presence with the angels. Know that this is promised to you. You need only accept. Stay close to me, my children., and I will surely and truly lead you to my Son.

I love you all, and I offer you my tender embraces and kisses. This is for each of you this day, my children. Continue your prayers and your fasting. Remain obedient, and love.

Good-bye.

---

[50] The final days of Lent, leading up to Good Friday

MESSAGE FROM MARY
APRIL 13, 1994

My beautiful children, I come to you today as the Queen of the Rosary—the Rosary, which is a sign of the victory of my Immaculate Heart. I thank you so for your diligence and your devotion to my prayer. I join them to mine as an offering to my Son, and to the Father Who loves you so.

My mission, children, the reason why I come in this fashion, is to prepare chosen souls for a special union with my Son. I speak often of my heart as a refuge for you, my children, as a place of safety. And I also prepare you to receive my Son into your hearts, to become one with His Sacred Heart, so that you can share His gospel message by the light of your lives, your pious duties, and the very example you set. Yes, you are being prepared for quiet suffering, but also immense joy, as you see my victory spread more and more.

Be not afraid to display your devotion to the most holy Rosary. It is an honor and a distinction that links you, in a very special way, to heaven and to my Son. It is truly a powerful prayer for the conversion of sinners and as an offering of reparation to the Father, Who is offended so deeply, Whose law of love is ignored by so many.

As my Son resided in my womb, so He existed in my heart. Before His birth, He graced by His presence all those with whom I came in contact. This participation is offered to all of you through the power of the Holy Spirit to share my Son's graces in a like manner. My children, pray for sinners. They need this prayer so desperately at this time. If you knew the pains of hell, the eternity of suffering that awaits those who turn away from my Son, who reject Him, reject His law of love, there is no sacrifice you would not be willing to make. Open your hearts to my Son, my children. Allow Him to reside there, find refuge from the blasphemy, the scourging, the pain and suffering with which the world attempts to make Him endure.

My children, know that I am always with you, that my angels watch over you continually. Be at peace. Find contentment in the knowledge of the part you play in the Father's grand design. I love you all so, and I leave you with my peace.

Good-bye, my children.

MESSAGE FROM MARY
APRIL 20, 1994

Children of God, my heart delights in your presence this day, and I am so grateful for all your prayers and the gift of this Rosary, which you pray so beautifully. It truly contributes to a great work and brings joy to so many.

My children, I am your guide to the Light, the Light Who is my Son, the Living God, one with the Father and the Holy Spirit. It is with His strength that I guide you and that I form you. Please be diligent in your cooperation with the spirit of preparation, which is bestowed on each of you. Your cooperation is through your prayers and your diligent search for truth—again, using your reason supported by my Son's Church. Always stay close to my heart. Do this through your prayers, your receipt of the Sacraments, and by listening and learning my Son's Word. My children, I love you so, and if you remain diligent, if you continue to strive for holiness, I will be your sure guide.

As I have told you so many times, there is much confusion, much dissention. At times, it seems the evil one is winning. But you now know, in your hearts, this is all illusion. The victory is won. My Son's love reigns eternal. Continue, my children, your prayers and supplications for God's mercy—that mercy so desperately needed by so many in the world who reject His offer.

I come with a Mother's hope that all my children will heed my Son; and it is this hope that you help me to build with your prayers and your sacrifices. My Son has promised that those who turn to Him will be helped with their burdens. Indeed, He will make the yoke light and gladden the heart. Do not press for more weight, my children. Be content with your place. Do not ask for crosses that are too heavy for you to bear.

Please know that this is a time of preparation, of strengthening, of fortification. Delight in the gifts I bring you. Be content, my children. Know the ship in which you ride is secure from the storm. Good-bye, my children. I leave each of you my blessing and a kiss of joy and love.

Good-bye.

MESSAGE FROM MARY
APRIL 22, 1994

My beautiful and faithful children, I thank you for coming together in this way. I thank you for sharing your lives as well as your prayers. You are truly becoming one in unity of purpose and love. My beautiful children, I come to you this evening with a special joy, for my Son, the King of Kings, the Lord of Lords, wishes to speak to you this evening. Please bow your heads for a short prayer, and I ask that you unite your hearts to mine:

Oh, glorious creation, glorious life. Oh, glorious love,
sing your praises to the Lord our God,
Unite in prayer and give praise to the Lord.

Almighty Savior, Your children welcome You.
Glory to God in the highest.
Peace on earth to all His children.

MESSAGE FROM JESUS

Children of God, it is I, your Lord, Who is with you this special evening. I thank you for honoring My Mother and for giving her such duty and devotion, praise, and love. If you hold steadfast, I tell you, you shall remain secure in her loving protection. You have gained her favor, My children, and because of this, you hold a special place in My heart.

You are called to spread the devotion to My Mother, but to do this in a very special way, a way that will show the power of the Holy Spirit. This is a way of love and gentle persuasion, of living the truths that I proclaim to the world. No matter the confusion, no matter the turmoil that you are subjected to, follow the hearts you have given to Me through My Mother. She will lead you to salvation, My children, because she leads you to Me, and I *am* salvation. I ask you to listen to My Mother, for she is the great teacher of hearts. There is no tender a love as the love of a Mother for her children; and you are her children.

Put aside your petty disputes. Keep your hearts clean, for a clean heart the enemy fears, and a cloudy heart blinds your eyes to the light. I ask you to take these words to heart, My children. Ponder on them. The lessons are true and food for your souls.

This evening I give you a special blessing and graces of perseverance and strength; and I warm each of your hearts, and I offer you the residence and security in My heart. *Please* invite Me, in return, My children, and be a witness to all those who ignore Me. In this way, you comfort My wounds and bring joy to My Mother, and I love My Mother joyful.

Good-bye, My children. Be at peace.

MESSAGE FROM MARY
APRIL 27, 1994

My beautiful children, it is I, your Mother, who speaks with you this day. I come to bring you my consolation and the grace of perseverance, and I offer you my strength for times of trial. This gift of my strength I freely give you.

My children, thank the Lord for your gift of faith. Thank Him for the hope that fills you, and thank Him for His love. It is on this love, my children, that you must build charity for all those who challenge you, for all those that lead you to despair, for all those who build anxiety and frustration. Many of them, my children, have good intentions. They operate in the light that God has seen to grant them, and they make their decisions as best they can.

Remember, the devil is *so* near. He tempts and he induces. His marks are fear, envy, hatred, and injustice. You know in your hearts when you confront him, and this, in itself, is a great grace because so many operate in darkness. So many this day know not the difference between good and evil, and much of this comes from man's pride, my children.

Though it is true that man's will is independent, he is still subject to so many forces. This independence has its limits, my children. If the will were not subject to these forces, then the will, itself, could impel perfection.

Love those who chastise you. Build your charity, for this is the greatest weapon I give you. In times of intense trial or stressful decision making, always look to my Son. He is the Good Shepherd. He is your strength. Stay loyal to the Church, my children. Obey the Holy Father,[51] I implore you. No matter

---

51 Message given during the pontificate of Pope John Paul II

the storms of confusion, no matter the doubts raised, stay home.

I love you all, my children, so much, and I leave you with my blessings.

Good-bye, my children.

MESSAGE FROM MARY
MAY 4, 1994

My beautiful children, it is I, your Mother, who speaks with you this day. Thank you, my children, for the gift of your Rosary. I hold these prayers to my heart, and I prepare them as an offering to my Son. I also thank you for coming to hear my words. Your perseverance, your consistency, warm my heart, for the words I speak to you are true, and they are given for your instruction and your support.

You are called to a grand purpose: to fulfill my Son's desire for the evangelization of so many. Oh! The sweetness of your witness, as it spreads through the purity of your lives, is a profound mystery to so many, and yet consoles so many. My children, always witness to what is holy. Be prepared always to sacrifice even the smallest point in order to maintain the clarity, the whiteness, and the beauty of your devotion.

The sacred, my children, must always be treated with reverence and respect, for that which is viewed and treated as common becomes common in the hearts of people. It pains me so to see so many who have devoted their lives to the Church treat my Son in the Blessed Sacrament in a common or trivial way, for you are spirit and body, my children. The spirit is influenced by the body, and if the body looks to my Son with indifference, if the actions and the attitudes portray indifference, the soul soon follows.

My children, I love you so, and the love my Son has for you is beyond measure. If only you could see the fullness of the great and glorious gift He has given you, the gift of Himself, the total and complete giving of God to His creatures.

I love you all, my children, so much—so very much, and I leave you with my blessing and a request . . . to share this love. Good-bye.

MESSAGE FROM MARY
MAY 11, 1994

My beautiful children, it is I, your Mother, who speaks with you this day. How beautiful it is that you meet in this holy place and so tenderly offer me your prayers. If only you could see how they assist me in washing the souls of so many of your brothers and sisters. What joy it brings me. What consolation for my heart pierced by the thorns of ingratitude, hatred, jealousy, and the distrust of my Son and His Church.

You have all been graced with special angels to protect you from so many things that may distract you from your purpose. What is your purpose, my children? To enter into salvation, to be with me in heaven, and to assist me during your stay in this world, in reparation for so many grievous sins. Heaven is such a beautiful place! Anxiety is replaced with perfect joy. Desire is replaced with perfect fulfillment. There is no longer hope, but acquisition. And faith is replaced with a perfect knowledge of the light that will fill you for all eternity. What beauty, what loveliness, what perfection in existence!

But until that time, my children, until the time of your resurrection, there is much to be done, much to accomplish. *Please, please,* remain diligent in the performance of your duties, those duties required by your vocation. Do not be distracted. Avoid busyness of all types. Learn your faith, my children. Understand what you can to the limit of your potential, and then allow the light to shine through you by your example and by your love. Stay with me. Find refuge in my Immaculate Heart. Know that I am always with you and that your angels will protect you. Pray at all times when decisions confront you. Be at peace.

Good-bye, my children.

MESSAGE FROM MARY
MAY 18, 1994

Beloved of God, my beautiful children, it is I, your Mother, who speaks with you this day. I wish to thank you for your constancy, your prayers of devotion, and your quiet suffering. The humble of heart, I love so dearly.

Today we meet between two great feasts[52]: one representing the promise; the other, endowing faith, hope, and charity. Imagine, if you will, my children, the blessed apostles praying quietly together in hopeful expectation of the fulfillment of my Son's promise. As the breath of God entered the room and the fire of the Holy Spirit touched their souls, they were made immediately capable of heroic virtue, the kind of virtue that ignited a faith that has circled the world.

My children, this gift of the Spirit is open to each of you. Ask and my Son will grant it. But it is the asking, the cooperation, that builds the Spirit within you. The apostles had faith, my children, but it was strengthened by the Spirit. They had hope, but it was taken to the heights of inexpressible joy. And they had love, but their charity was increased to include all mankind, especially charity for themselves. My children, forgive yourselves. Don't be harsh. This is a stumbling block for so many and makes it so very difficult for you to look beyond the faults of others.

Be at peace. Pray to the Father, to the Son, to the Holy Spirit, that the flame of faith, hope, and charity may expand in you. This great gift, given to you at your baptism, can grow to such heights, my children, with your cooperation. And this cooperation is so important because I wish you all to be

---

[52] Ascension and Pentecost

ambassadors and apostles for my Son. Share with those sent to you. Give them my words of peace and hope and joy. *But test the spirit.*

My children, there is so much I wish to share with you about the joy and exultation of that day so long ago. But the same is offered to you, my children. My arms are open, always ready to hold you, to lead you to my Son.

Good-bye, my children. I love you all so much.

MESSAGE FROM MARY
MAY 25, 1994

My children, it is I, your Mother, who speaks with you this day. Prepare yourselves well, my children. Pray, fast, do penance. Remain dutiful and obedient. Assist at Mass. Receive the Sacraments as often as possible. Through all these gifts, you will come closer to my Son and find refuge there from all the storms that this life may bring.

I have told you so many times about the enemy and his destructive behavior throughout the world. All of you are a special challenge to him. He lusts after your hearts. He promises you security, comfort, the avoidance of pain, wealth, prestige—whatever will work to steer you off course, to blind you, and to keep you from your destiny . . . a destiny in which he can never partake.

My children, my Immaculate Heart is always open to you. I am always there for those who consecrate themselves to me. And if you suffer, it is for the salvation of souls and to secure in you the knowledge and the desire to look after things that are not of this world. A time is soon coming, my children, when this will truly be all that matters to you. Stay close to me and know that I will always stay close to you.

I love you, and I leave you now with my maternal blessings and abundant graces that come from my Son. All glory to God. He is the Most High. Good-bye.

MESSAGE FROM MARY
JUNE 1, 1994

My beautiful children, it is I, your tender Mother of Mercy, who speaks with you now. I offer you my love and my protection, and I thank you for your beautiful prayers. A Rosary, such as yours, brings delight to my pierced heart. There is so much strength, my children, in your prayer, and it is with joy that I tell you that my Son has granted consent for your special protection.

My children, I wish to lead you to sainthood, to the commitment that leads to "the bliss," the only true bliss, the presence of the Ever-Living and Almighty Creator of all that is. For many of you, it will be a long and arduous journey, fraught with dangers and temptations. But these will also be times filled with joy in the knowledge of your participation in the salvation of so many.

The nations truly rage against Our Lord and all His baptized children, those anointed with a portion of the burden of the Cross. Oh, my children, the Church's martyrdom is the same as my Son's, and it manifests itself in three distinct ways: a martyrdom of blood, a martyrdom of message unheeded, and a martyrdom of holiness spurned and ridiculed. My children, *this must be*. But know that you are protected with my loving embrace and that as long as you respond to the call of my Son's heart, there will be no room in you for the enemy, for my Son fills all.

Be at peace, my children. Continue in your devotions. Watch and pray, for this is the time. Good-bye.

MESSAGE FROM MARY
JUNE 8, 1994

My beautiful children, it is I, your Mother, who speaks with you this day. I bring you joy, the joy of your salvation and the hope that you will reside with me by the side of my Son. The glory that awaits you at the end of your trials is impossible to describe, but I promise to touch your hearts with a taste of this bliss at times when you are in most need.

Open your hearts, my children. Let me comfort them. Let me console you as you approach the test. My Mother's love wishes to conceal you from all that can do you harm, to protect you from injustice, to shade you from the hatred of this world. These flames begin to fan, and at times, you feel as if they will consume you. I ask that you trust and that you have faith and confidence in your Mother, who loves you so.

I have asked you many times to test the spirit, what lies behind your endeavors or those challenges you meet. To feel dry or distant, to feel lonely—these, my children, are signs of your growth. Offer them to me so that I may take them to my Son. What you must test for, my children, are feelings of despair, envy, insidious hatred, for these destroy your growth and are handholds that crumble. My path is filled with peace, regardless of the storms that rage outside you. Always look to me, my children, and look to my Son. Be at peace, and know that I shelter you with my tender caress.

Good-bye.

MESSAGE FROM MARY
JUNE 15, 1994

My children, you are truly of God, and I thank you for your prayers, the fragrance of which accompanies me to the court of heaven. Be at peace. Still your hearts. When you meet with me in this way, leave the cares of the world behind, and immerse yourselves in your prayers of consecration and devotion.[53]

My children, pursue the way of the Lord with humility. You must imitate Him and pray constantly for virtue. Self-imposed mortifications are truly beneficial, only if they bring joy, and the joy of which I speak is not a boisterous or emotional one, but rather a quiet joy that comes with the knowledge that you are very close to God. My children, if mortifications—these sufferings and gifts to my Son's Cross—do not bring this joy, know that perhaps it is not God's will that you endure these. Find joy in the crosses that our God provides. When you give your lives totally to me, when you truly trust in Our Lord Jesus, you will live for this day. Yesterday and tomorrow are heaven's concern.

I love you all so dearly, and I give you my tender and maternal blessings and gentle caresses. Good-bye, my children.

---

[53] The cenacle renewed its consecration to Mary at each gathering by reciting a formal prayer of consecration before praying the Rosary.

MESSAGE FROM MARY
JUNE 22, 1994

My children, my beautiful and loving children, continue with your devout prayers and your constant receipt of the Sacraments, for these are the waters that will quench your parched souls as you continue on your journeys. Continue to join your sufferings and your trials to my Son's Cross, and know that they contribute, in a way that you cannot understand, to the strength and glory of the Church.

My children, in Scripture, the man Samson prefigures my Son, for in the tragedy of his passion and death, he proves strongest. In a special way, this man's life also prefigures the life of the Church. His strength was awesome, renowned in defense of truth and God's children. He destroyed much evil. But he was seduced, his vision impaired, his hair shorn. The world ridiculed him, blasphemed him, and heaped abuse after abuse upon his person. But all the while, his hair began to grow, and the Spirit swelled within him. And at the height of his rejection and his ridicule, his debasement and torture, he pitted his great strength against the twin pillars of pride and unbelief that support the world's iniquities. And in the culmination of his agony, he destroyed more evil in his death than he did in his life.

Look to the signs of the times, my children, and understand. Be joyful, for the glorious reign of my Son is at hand. I love you all, and I leave you with my peace and abundant blessings.

Good-bye, my children.

MESSAGE FROM MARY
JUNE 29, 1994

Beautiful children of God, and my children, it is I, your Mother, who speaks with you this day. I offer you the tender mercy of my Son, Our Lord and our Savior.

What a glorious plan of God, the Resurrection of my Son, the Being made whole, death defeated. My children, the enemy's name is Division. He divides families, he divides peoples and nations, he divides creature and Creator, and he divides all of you. He *has* asked to sift you like wheat, and I pray for you, that your faith remains strong. Oh, the Resurrection of my Son . . . the glory of the Almighty's plan.

My children, Satan hates the physical world. That which he considers his greatest triumph was the division of your bodies from your souls at death. That was his shallow victory. He hates God so, my children, and he especially hates you. He hates you so because you represent the salvation of so many.

When my Son was crucified, the devil thought Him sent back to dust, with his victory remaining complete. But oh, that glorious third day! That is God's gift, my children. That is the greatness of His plan. For my Son is the firstborn of all creation. With your bodies and souls united as whole beings, you will enjoy the blessings, the favor, the presence, and the vision of the Almighty, Who is from everlasting to everlasting.

Persevere in your prayers, my children. Remain strong in your devotions. Pray and fast so that my Son's light may shine through you. I offer your hearts to Him constantly, and in this way, you are purified through me to carry this light. I thank you for your consecrations and your offerings of your hearts. They are so precious to me.

I love you all, and please remember that I pray for all of you. Good-bye, my children.

MESSAGE FROM MARY
JULY 6, 1994

My beautiful children, it is I, your Mother, who speaks to you this day through my servant. Be at peace and rest your hearts in my immaculate embrace. Know that I care for each of you tenderly, and I enclose each of your hearts in my special petition to my Holy Son.

My children, you are all called to participate in the supreme martyrdom, that martyrdom which was the offering of my Son on the Cross for all of you. It was supreme in that it was the martyrship of God. God, Himself, experienced death for all of you. How, my children, do you participate in this martyrdom? You do this by assenting to the Father's will. It is in this and only this, from which all true martyrdom springs. By assenting to His will, you participate, in a very real way, with my Son in the blessings and merits He has earned for you. What a glorious mystery, my children, that in offering Himself to the world for humiliation, torture, rejection, and intense pain of body and spirit, He would glorify God, Himself, and all of humanity joined with Him, through Him, and in Him.

All glory and praise to our God, my children. Sing His praises in your heart. Know that I love you and that I am with you always, even to the sacrifice of my only Son. Good-bye, my children

MESSAGE FROM MARY
JULY 13, 1994

My beautiful children, it is I, your tender Mother, who prays and speaks with you this day. So blessed are you, my children, to have the life of Jesus within you, to be in His Heart, where no harm can befall you.

He has given you a great gift, my children, the gift of His teachings through His Vicar[54] and the apostles joined with him. It is your beacon to guide you through the mists of confusion and pride—especially pride, the downfall of so many of my children.

The Spirit picked all of you, my children, from time immemorial; but my Son picked twelve, and the Father picked one.[55] That one, and his successors, speak for my Son, and they speak for me. Hear and obey! . . . for there is your refuge.

A flood of dissention, of pride, rebellion, covers the earth, and the earth drinks it to its fill.[56] But you, my children, are protected in my mantle. You are with me at the foot of the Cross. Pray for those who, through misunderstanding, rebellion—all due to pride, stray away. So very soon they will come to realize what they have done, how they have misunderstood, and they will gather around me. My brood will come home and await the joyous resurrection of my Son's Church.

I love you all, my children, so dearly, and I give you each my special blessing this day. I lay my hands upon you and

---

[54] This is most likely a reference to the newly released *Catechism of the Catholic Church*.

[55] One may assume that our Blessed Mother is referring to the Gospel passage in Matthew 16:13-19.

[56] Revelation 12:14-16

anoint you with the affection of my Immaculate Heart. Good-bye, my children.

MESSAGE FROM JESUS
JULY 20, 1994

Children of My Mother, you are the third measure of flour[57] that I give to her. I give you to her so that she may apply the leaven of My graces, and to mold and knead you until you have fully risen. This is to prepare you for the end of the age[58] and to unite you as My special children with My Mother.

I tell you this: *through her* all My graces flow to the world. This was made manifest at My death, when at the foot of My Cross, I poured out My graces and abundant blessings through her Immaculate and Sorrowful Heart to My beloved apostle John, who represents all of you and the Church, Herself, in this matter.

Why was John My beloved apostle? Why did I hold him so dear to My Heart and allow him the rest and repose of My breast? This is mentioned for no other apostle. Why? Because in a special and unique way, at the foot of the Cross, he was fully united with My Mother's Immaculate and Sorrowful Heart. This is the great gift and blessing I bestow on you: the honor to be fully consumed in My Mother's majesty and there share My glory. In sharing this glory, you are unique among all creatures.

As God created man, God was born of man. As God is pure Spirit, God shares your body, your soul, your will. This entails My glorious plan, children. I tell you this and

---

[57] **Third measure of flour:** this language most surely refers to the parable told by Jesus in the Gospels of Luke 13:20-21 and Matthew 13:33, describing the Kingdom of Heaven. Walter was led to understand through the Spirit that the "three measures of flour" represent the three parts of the Church; the Church Triumphant in Heaven, the Church Suffering in Purgatory, and we, the Church Militant here on earth. In this message today, Jesus is telling us that Mary is the woman of the parable who applies the leaven of His graces to the whole Church.

[58] Matthew 13:39-40, 49

announce this to you so you will not misunderstand. Be Johns. Stay close to My Mother. Accept this call. Stay at the foot of My Cross. Mourn for the souls in purgatory. Continue your prayers and sacrifices. I love you all as children of God, and I leave you with My blessings. Good-bye, My children.

MESSAGE FROM MARY
JULY 27, 1994

My beautiful children, it is I, your Mother, who speaks with you this day. What a marvelous gift, your beautiful prayers. They are truly a great weapon against sin and the destruction to which the enemy tries to drive so many souls. When you pray in this fashion,[59] it is a soothing balm for my Immaculate Heart, which is so badly pierced by the sorrow of the world.

I wish this day to ask something very special of all of you. I wish you to spread these cenacles. Start them among your families. Pray the Rosary as I have taught you, and lead it with my consecration. If you do this, my children, the benefits to yourselves and the sinners of the world will be immeasurable.

The enemy will try very hard to dissuade this effort. He will distract your family members. You will notice certain tensions, trials, and frustrations, at the time you have designated [for family prayer]. Be steadfast and humble. Intimidate or attempt to force no one. If it starts with just you and a small child—even just a decade, if need be—that is all that's necessary. For I tell you, in this way the seed is planted, the grain is sown, and from this field will come a great harvest.

I know all your concerns, my children, your fears and anxieties. Do not become preoccupied with the future. Live for today. Fulfill those commitments that are presented to you, and seek the Kingdom of God. If you do this, all that you need will be given to you.

---

[59] The cenacle prayed the Rosary as if they were speaking directly to Our Blessed Mother, with love and reverence, slowly, softly, and gently.

I love you all, and I leave you with my maternal blessing.

Good-bye.

MESSAGE FROM MARY
AUGUST 3, 1994

My beautiful children, it is I, your Mother, the Mother of Miracles and Mercies, who speaks with you this day. I bring you the peace of my Son. Let it fill your hearts and numb your pain. You must protect yourselves, children. Be vigilant against the errors of the times. Know that the Spirit is with you and will help you.

My children, the miraculous works of my Son were a great proof that He was Who He said He was,[60] and continues to be the only Son of God, one with the Father and the Spirit, Whom They sent. My Son's many miracles were as signs to the world of His benevolence and His mercy. He healed the sick, He raised the dead, He walked on the waters, and He fed the multitudes. This meal was a symbol, a sign of the Paschal Meal[61] to be offered in memorial of Him, until His return. To this meal, you bring nothing of yourselves except faith and a contrite heart.

The Bread of Life was a free gift, solely given by my Son; and it is this truth, it is this great victory that the enemy tries to hide or destroy. He explains it away in the natural order, or he ascribes to it a human involvement that does not exist. At the root of this denial is the denial of Who my Son said He was—in short, a denial of God.

You must pray, my children, for those who fall by the wayside, who confuse the truth, who hide behind the mirage of utopian[62] potential. Stay with the Truth, my children. It sets your spirits free. It has been revealed and can be known by

---

[60] **The miraculous works of Jesus (John 5:36-37):** That week, many of the local priests in various parishes attempted to offer natural explanations in their Sunday homilies for the multiplication of the loaves and fishes and other miracles.

[61] **Paschal Meal:** the Holy Sacrifice of the Mass

[62] **Utopian:** proposing or advocating ideal social and political schemes that are impractical; having impossibly ideal conditions; one that believes in the perfectibility of human society.

you. Listen to your hearts, for the Spirit is there. Always turn to my Son's Church and the teachings of His Vicar[63] and those who are in union with him.

You are to be vanguards of the Truth, my children. Hold this light precious. Be careful and sparing in its use, for this is a time of darkness, and the light is not understood.

Good-bye, my children. I love you all, and I leave you with my peace.

---

[63] Message given during the pontificate of Pope John Paul II

MESSAGE FROM MARY
AUGUST 10, 1994

My beautiful children, it is I, your Mother, the Mother of Infinite Mercy, who speaks with you this day. Be at peace. Rest secure in the knowledge of God's love. It brings such joy to my Sorrowful Heart to see you together praying in this fashion to the Blessed Trinity. Your hearts truly swell with infused virtue at times like this.

What glory you bring to the Father, and to the Son, and to Their Spirit. I assure you, for every ounce of love you share amongst yourselves or give to the world, a pound is returned to you. You will not be left lacking in any grace, my children, if you implore the name of my Son.

What a glorious gift it was for Him to share our nature and to affect our redemption. It is to salvation you are all heading, my children. And through God's grace, you will run the race to the finish[64] and be with Him in paradise to enjoy the vision of His beauty, and to be as God yourselves—not in substance, but in likeness. This, too, shows the greatness of God's plan, because in this way, you will retain your individual personage, your love of self and of each other.

It is written that upon my Son's return, He will bring death and avenge the blood of the martyrs.[65] My children, this is not the death of those perpetrators, for that [death] is their free choice. Rather, He will bring death to sin's motivation, that concupiscence that separates you from unity with all heaven. What a glorious triumph this final victory will be. And as I mediated for you so long ago, I ask you to "do as He

---

[64] 1 Corinthians 9:24-27

[65] Book of Revelation 6:10

tells you to do." In this way, you will share the best wine together.[66]

I love you all, my children, and I leave you with my Son's abundant graces; and know that I cherish you always. Good-bye.

---

[66] Our Blessed Mother is surely referring to the Gospel account of the Wedding Feast at Cana in John 2:1-11. In our times, she observes the Church's need and again intercedes for us, saying to her Son, "They have no more wine." Another possible reference might be found in Acts 2:13, wherein the apostles receive the gift of the Holy Spirit at Pentecost and are accused of "being full of new wine." Our Blessed Mother seems to be saying that the "best wine" is yet to come for the Church: a great outpouring of the Holy Spirit.

MESSAGE FROM MARY
AUGUST 17, 1994

My beautiful children, it is I, your Mother, who speaks with you this day, and I come to you as the Mother of Special Protection. Fill your hearts with zeal, my children, for the Father, and the Son, and the Holy Spirit.

Embrace the cross. Do not fear it, for the cross is the source of all your treasures in heaven. In these times, avoid the devil's greatest snare of allurement. This snare is built around the self—self-awareness, self-fulfillment. These terms are contradictions, my children, and they are lies, for the harder they are strived after, the more confused and disappointed and disillusioned the soul becomes. And it is at these times that the enemy piles on even more intrusions. *Only through God, my children, is there fulfillment, and that path always leads to the cross.*

The time soon comes when my Son will cleanse the temple,[67] and I offer you my special protection, and I offer you the ability to reside in my heart. There, you will unite with my Son, for it is also His abode.

My children, pray especially for those souls who receive my Son [in the Blessed Sacrament] in a state of grave sin. My children, please understand, at this time you are united truly with my Son, body and soul, and for those who do not understand, they participate in driving the spikes, in wielding the whips. And my Son prays constantly for them: "Father, they know not what they do."[68]

Through my Son's abundant love, you are made my children. This means that when you are in pain, turn to me . . . know that I am with you. When you suffer humiliation or

---

[67] The Church
[68] Luke 23:34

rejection, again, turn to me, for I am there to comfort you and to protect you. In my heart, children, is the only peace, because in my heart, resides my Son. Come to me when your souls are sick, when strength and happiness elude you, and know that my arms are always open.

Good-bye, my children. I love you.

MESSAGE FROM MARY
AUGUST 24, 1994

My sweet and beautiful children, I speak to you this day as the Mother of Divine Mercy, and I thank you for your wonderful gift. This act of consecration, which I have given you, together with your prayers, are used for a great work. You may ask my chosen one what he has been shown to explain this.[69]

I am the grape, my children, from which flowed the new wine of redemption. And you are asked not just to drink this cup, but to fill it yourselves. I was the first fruits, but you are *all* called to be the harvest of the Father. Though it is true that you must be pressed to extract your contribution, it is a joyous process. The true press is my Son's Cross. And you all contribute in your special ways to fill the "cup of salvation"— one cup, one body, in total union.

My children, Our Lord is much distressed at the sin and suffering in the world. In reparation, you must pray constantly for all the souls suffering in delusion and despair. Receive the Sacraments. Participate prayerfully in the Holy Mass. Be obedient to the Holy Father[70] and the magisterium of his Church.

My children, the Church belongs to the Holy Father as a vessel belongs to its captain. The true owners hire this captain

---

[69] Walter was shown an interior vision today, during the Rosary, of a desolate place, grayish in color, strewn with large rocks and boulders and covered with a dense fog. This vision brought about deeply painful feelings of emptiness and intense sorrow. However, in the distance a very bright and warm light was visible, which stirred up feelings of great hope and joy. As our cenacle prayed each Hail Mary prayer, a shadowy silhouette in the shape of a person was seen to rise from below and move slowly toward the beautiful light. Our Blessed Mother conveyed to Walter that this interior vision was of purgatory, and our prayers were being used this day to release souls to heaven.

[70] Message given during the pontificate of Pope John Paul II

so that he may see the ship's cargo safely to port. Avoid those who talk of mutiny, for it leads to shipwreck and disaster.

I love you all, my children, so dearly, and I give you my tender embrace and an abundance of my Son's blessings. Good-bye, my children.

MESSAGE FROM MARY
AUGUST 31, 1994

My beloved and beautiful children, it is I, your Mother, who speaks with you this day. I thank you for your intentions, for the gift of your prayers and sacrifices. Please continue earnestly in all you do to allow the light of my Son to be seen in you.

My children, so long ago, my Son died on the Cross, causing many reactions. Some fled in fear. Others denied in anguish and disgust. Most saw only a man, and these, in particular, ignored my presence. But there I was, adoring and offering, and I do this even today.[71]

After His Resurrection, my Son said these words: "Blessed are they who do not see, but believe."[72] And for those filled with this grace, He would give a sign, the sign of His body. Those blest saw His body on the Cross as the glory of God. To this day, when the priest says, "This is my body," those blest see the glory of God. My children, pray for those who saw only a man, and pray for those who see only bread.

I love you all so much, and this love is the love of a tender Mother and the love of a spouse, because I love all and am a part of all that is of God. And from eternity, you are all the thought of God, created above all to share in His life. What glory! What blessed honor!

My Son is always with you, but especially in the Tabernacles. It is there that my angels are always assembled in adoration. It is there that I am by His side, as I was at the

---

[71] Our Blessed Mother surely implies that the people today who do not see Our Lord's Presence in the form of bread are also those who ignore her role in our salvation. The reverse of this may be true also.

[72] Ref: John 20:29

Cross. He sacrifices for you, my children. He feeds you. And to be present, He allows Himself voluntarily to be imprisoned. It is a tomb[73] of joy, my children. Please partake. Examine your conscience,[74] pray and simply adore in His presence, as often as your duties allow. Together with Communion and the Sacraments of the Church, you will be protected from all that can befall you, and the enemy can never touch you. Of this, I give you my promise and the guarantee from my Son. Good-bye, my children. I love you all.

---

[73] **Tomb:** a place of internment; a place for the burial of the dead. Our Lady seems to be saying that just as Jesus remained God in the sepulchre, after his bloody sacrifice on the Cross, so He remains God in the Tabernacle after the Sacrifice of the Mass.

[74] Following the message, Our Blessed Mother privately explained to Walter that when we examine our conscience in the presence of Our Lord in the Tabernacle, we are able to see a truer picture of ourselves because our pride is more easily broken down, and we are more protected from scruples and the devil's false accusations.

MESSAGE FROM MARY
SEPTEMBER 7, 1994

My beautiful children, it is your Mother, and the Mother of your Lord, who speaks with you now. Let my love fill you, so there is room for nothing else. This love will empty you of all diversions, all prides and jealousies. It will remove ambitions and all hatred. There will be no room for envy or jealousy. An abundant space will be created, and this space is promised to be filled by my Son. His Eucharist, my children, is so powerful in its love, and it is with this that I wish you to be filled. He longs for you so, my children. He waits in darkness, in the Tabernacles of the world, for consolation and the joy of your respectful presence.

It is for love that you were created. It is in love that you will end. But this "end" will go on for eternity . . . an eternity of bliss you cannot comprehend. Find joy in the small things . . . and happiness in the presence of others. The more my love fills you, the more of my Son you will see in each person.

Be diligent in your prayers. Attend Mass as often as you can. Return my Son's love. This is important, my children, in these times, for in these times you are being prepared for trials and challenges. I wish you to know that soon I will not be with you in this way as often, and so I ask you to heed my words and pull close to my Son. I will show the way.

Be at peace now. I leave you with my caresses and the love of your Mother. Good-bye, my children.

MESSAGE FROM MARY
SEPTEMBER 14, 1994

My beautiful children so full of love, it is I, your Mother, who speaks with you this day. Be at peace and find comfort in the mystery of the Cross,[75] the very Cross to which my heart was transfixed in union with my Son, for the redemption of the world.

The debt was paid. The Sacrifice was made, the Sacrifice of God and man, in unity. In unity, God shares all with you, and you are called to share all with Him. The Cross is a work of love and a great mystery of redemption, and to this Cross all are called. The darkness cannot understand it, for the darkness cannot see love.

Oh, my children, our God loves us so, that He came into the world to sacrifice on your behalf. But to find union with Him, you are all called to participate. Your burdens, each and every one, are carried for the love of God; and when you are finally transfixed in union with Him, God will truly fill you. The real and true presence of this Sacrifice is always with you. And this Sacrifice, if received with love, fills and consumes you with its fire and prepares you to receive the divine presence . . . the very presence for which you were created.

I leave you now, my children, and I offer you a goodly portion of my Son's love. Partake with confidence, and know that He is always with you. Good-bye.

---

[75] This day was the feast day of the Triumph of the Cross.

MESSAGE FROM MARY
SEPTEMBER 21, 1994

My beautiful children, it is I, your Mother, who speaks with you this day. I am truly in your presence, and I bless each and every one of you. I caress you, and I pray to God for what is best for your souls.

The Truth is wondrous news to a world enveloped in darkness, the blindness of pride, and this blindness is the most effective means the enemy has to darken souls. But be not in fear of the winter, for spring shall soon arrive. The door has been opened, and the path lays before you. I will assist you along this glorious and beautiful path. Its brightness expels the dark and slowly cleanses your souls and prepares them for their destination.

Your chief weapons against this demon of pride, my children, are prayer, fasting, the Sacraments of Holy Mother Church, and the grace of an intense desire for humility. Cultivate this, my children, for this demon truly prowls about you, and he leaps at the slightest invitation. Pray that all you do, all serious endeavors, are united to and work through the will of God. Self-will bears bad fruit, and it always ends with mouths full of dust and hearts heavy with despair.

A sure test as to whether you truly do the Father's will is not necessarily challenges, for good and evil are always in opposition; even evil is challenged. Look, rather, to what those challenges produce in you and those around you. If those challenges produce anxiety, envy, hatred, jealousies, frustrations, know that in this, the Father's will is not present. But if it produces sorrow, a desire for healing, a concern for others, and a quiet humility and trust that God's will be done . . . these are the good signs. I do not mean that you must not persevere against challenges. This is always needed, my children, for to do the will of the Father is always difficult. But

I give you these tests to search your hearts and to beg our God for what is needed.

I leave you now, my children, with my blessings, and I thank you for your prayers and your devotion. Good-bye.

MESSAGE FROM MARY
SEPTEMBER 28, 1994

My beautiful children, it is I, your Mother, who speaks with you this day. You comfort my heart with your prayers and the sincerity of your souls.

Though some of you may be distracted at times, your efforts and your trials against these distractions will not go unrewarded. You pray for the gifts of the Spirit, and I assure you, the greatest of these has been showered upon you. This gift is the gift of His love. It permeates the very atmosphere you breathe and unites you all in one beautiful song of praise to the Father.

Most of you know this, my children. You feel the peace that this love brings when you meet here, and you know that what I say is true. But for some who do not feel this peace and consolation, please know that this love pours in them abundantly all the more. This love is like a balm, a sweet, fragrant oil. It removes the dirt and grime that this world presses on so many of you. Over time, this cleansing action purifies the surface and penetrates deep within, to preserve from all infection all the harmful effects that the world can press upon you.

You are all created in the image of God, and in this you reflect Him. Each of you as an individual are a special reflection of the Creator. How can you not be loved? . . . for there is none like you before, and there will be none like you ever again. The Spirit of Love is an immensity so infinite that God can fill you each to a measure beyond knowing. I promise you, through the Spirit you will find peace in your trials, strength in your battles, and courage from the most fearful confrontations. Allow this love to fill you, and know that as it does, you increase in holiness . . . this holiness which is goodness and lovability . . . this goodness which does the will of the Father.

Be at peace, my children, and know that I love you all so dearly. Please know that my angels' wings will bring you to safety and protect your loved ones.

Good-bye, my children.

MESSAGE FROM MARY
OCTOBER 5, 1994

My beautiful children, it is I, your Mother, the Mother of your Lord, and I bring to you this day an offer of a great gift.

Please come closer to me, love me dearly, and I will lead you to my Son. I wish you to come so close in spirit that I can hand your hearts to Him. You may come closer to me, my children, by increasing your devotion and your adoration of the Eucharist in the Tabernacle or on exposition, but especially at the Sacrifice of the Mass. Pray for faith and for strength to believe, because the Eucharist is the source of all your strength, all your power, and the glory to which you are destined.

Everywhere, my Son's doctrines are under attack, and the strongest weapon you have is your faith and devotion. Come close, my children. Open your hearts because by the grace of my Son, I merit roses for my prayers and my suffering, and I wish to place one in each of your hearts. This is my gift to you, my children, and the great secret of your Rosaries, because when you receive my Son, you are consumed in the flame of His love, and there He finds in your heart my rose—my prayers and my sufferings. And He finds these most dear.[76]

---

[76] Walter saw an interior vision, wherein an angel was poised above people who received the Eucharist. The angel carried in his hands a beautiful sensor into which he gathered their offerings, sufferings and prayers, in communion with Christ. These were then consumed in the flame of Our Lord's love and carried to heaven. It seems our Blessed Mother is telling us that if we come closer to her by increasing our devotion to the Eucharist, she will place a rose, merited by *her* prayers and sufferings, into our hearts; and this rose, her gift to us, will be consumed along with our prayers, as an offering to our Heavenly Father. There is no more wonderful a gift that can be given to God than the prayers and sufferings of Mary, united with the Eucharistic sacrifice of Jesus. What a tremendous blessing we have been offered!

No matter what trials come your way, no matter the strength of the storm, rest secure in this knowledge, and maintain your focus on my Son in the Blessed Sacrament. It pleases me so, my children, to give you this gift, and I leave you now with my love and abundant blessings.

Good-bye, my children.

MESSAGE FROM MARY
October 12, 1994

Beautiful children of God, I greet you with my maternal affection, and I thank you for your prayers and sacrifices. Your continual consecrations warm my heart and are put to great use: the salvation of so many souls.

These are times of confusion and terrible disarray. I know that at times you feel that you don't know which way to turn. Find security and shelter in the Eucharist, my children, for there the abundance of grace exists on this planet, in this world; and for love of you, my Son continues to offer Himself.

Pray for those children who do not know me and do not know my Son, those that deny the Eucharist, those that accuse my Son's Vicar[77] of fighting the work of the Holy Spirit, those that would deny you the Sacraments or obscure their benefits, those that through the pride of rebellion would undermine my work and the sacrifice of so many of my Son's martyrs. Pray for God's mercy, my children, for they do not know God, and only in knowing God is the grace of salvation received—for in receiving that grace, knowledge of God fills the heart.

Please be at peace, my children. I know these times try your resolve and your confidence. Know that with every Rosary, every prayer of true devotion, you build the walls of the fortress—stone by stone. That means salvation for so many.

Good-bye, my children. Please continue your prayers, your fasting, and your penance. Offer them to my Son continually. Good-bye.

---

[77] Pope John Paul II

184

MESSAGE FROM MARY
OCTOBER 26, 1994

My beautiful children, it is I, your Mother, who speaks with you this day. Let your spirits remain calm, and join with me in entering the Sacred Heart of my Son. There, is the seat of all virtue; there, is the source of all goodness and strength; and there, you will find perseverance for the trials of darkness that soon come.

To the capacity that your duties allow, spend time with my Son. Pray with me before Him in the Blessed Sacrament, and engage your souls with the mystery of the Cross. There, you will learn wisdom; there, you will muster the energy you need to fulfill your duties, to discern for decision making, and to feed your souls.

My children, the Son is a loving ruler. What he has prepared for those who persevere is beyond human comprehension. Holy doctrine only touches on the magnificence that awaits you, my children. My little ones, stay with me and I will share my crown with you, and together we will be in the joyful presence of the Trinity . . . forever.

Be at peace and call on me in times of decision. Measure every act against the good example set in the Gospel. Be prepared always to ask for forgiveness so that you may bathe in my Son's light. Good-bye, my children. Please know that I love you all so dearly, and I come to each of you now with a special caress.

MESSAGE FROM MARY
NOVEMBER 2, 1994

My beautiful children, it is I, your Mother, the Mother of Holy Souls,[78] who speaks with you this day. Together with the prayers of the whole Church, you have helped to free so many from the pains of purgation.

All souls in the Church Suffering see the face of God and are then deprived. This is so severe, my children. They are secure in their salvation . . . and they hunger and thirst for my Son's divine presence in a way you could not imagine. My Son knew of this pain in the garden. He felt it intimately.

I love you all so much, and my whole heart's desire is to lead you to my Son to enjoy His light and His life. The Church Suffering knows this. Their love for you is immense, and they pray for you often. Many of your relatives, whose names you do not know from past generations, love you with an intense flame, and they pray for your salvation. Will you pray for them, my children—the many souls who are forgotten so much of the year?

I say again, they suffer because they lack my Son's presence. This [presence] is a great gift for all of you. His hands are so close to you. His benevolence surrounds you. But your souls are clouded. You do not see this. But this is the walk of faith, my children; and as the veil is pulled away upon your deaths, you will see Truth in all its magnificence, and rejoice.

Be at peace and rest secure in the knowledge of my Son's love for all of you. Good-bye, my children.

---

[78] This day was the Feast of All Souls.

MESSAGE FROM MARY
NOVEMBER 9, 1994

Beautiful children of God, it is I , your Mother, who speaks with you this day. I thank you for your beautiful prayers. I implore you to continue them with diligence, for they effect a great change in the hearts of men.

My children, how I love to gather you in the arms of my cenacles, for it is here you join so many of my children—children who pray for my Son's return. The time is imminent, the harvest is ready, but know that in His Heart is a place for each of you. I know, my children, it's hard to say yes to His Heart, and even harder to back up this yes with the actions required to verify it. But know that this is possible only through grace, a grace I pray to give you each and every day.

Though some of you may go wayward from time to time, remember the story of the "Prodigal,"[79] and know that this is a continuous process, for the Father's mercy is abundant and without measure.

Treat the peace I give you as treasure, my children. Store it safely in your hearts. Protect it. If you do this, you will avoid despair and disillusionment, and you will find it easier to discern my Son's will for you.

Be at peace. Prepare your hearts, as you all await the "cleansing of the temple."[80] Good-bye, my children.

---

[79] Luke 15:11-32
[80] The cleansing of the Church

MESSAGE FROM MARY
NOVEMBER 23, 1994

My beautiful children, it is I, your Mother, who speaks with you this day, and I ask you to give thanks[81] to God, for He is all good, and His love for each of you endures forever.

What does this mean, my children? It means the blood He shed, the life He gave, makes you worthy. One drop of His blood, His holy and precious blood, could save an infinity of souls. Such is His power. But it was shed for you—for you, my children—so that you may see salvation and come to know the Father.

In Jesus Christ you are made worthy. To deny this is to blaspheme His blood. Yes, you are unworthy in yourselves; but in my Son, your garments are made white and you are capable of all glory. Respond to His grace, my children, for His grace is a grace of perfect love, and perfect love cleanses perfectly. Be joyful in your exaltation. Be thankful for the Lamb that has made you worthy.

Meditate on all of this, my children, for it should be your guidepost between presumption and despair. Know that the devil works at you. When you fall, when you harm others, he accuses you. Do you doubt my Son's blood? Then accept His forgiveness. I love you all, and I leave you now with my blessing.

Good-bye, my children.

---

[81] The following day was Thanksgiving Day.

MESSAGE FROM MARY
NOVEMBER 30, 1994

My beautiful children, I am the Mother of Consolation, and I am truly with you this day. Let my Son's peace fill your hearts. May you be totally enveloped in His love.

My children, I never tire of thanking you for your prayers. Do not tire in offering them to me. Remain resolute and steadfast in your devotions. My Son, Our Lord, has promised me that you will be filled with these graces, if you ask. He is truly the Lord of Lords and the King of Kings, but He is also your brother, and He shares all of your concerns.

I ask you to take your daily concerns to Him—your plans, your successes and failures. Lay them before Him. Speak to Him. I assure you He is the best of listeners, and your hearts will never go away empty or devoid of His consolation. You may not feel it, but I assure you it is there.

I must stress with you this day, my children, that this is a time of preparation, a time of strengthening. For soon, St. Michael comes with the sword of Truth, and his sword will pierce every heart and bind the wounds.

My children, there is so much I wish to share with you, but it is enough for you to know this day that I am always near, always the faithful guide who leads the way to your Savior . . . and mine. Good-bye, my children. I love you.

MESSAGE FROM JESUS
DECEMBER 7, 1994

Peace to you, sons and daughters of Mary! I come to announce that the fulfillment of joy is at hand. And I ask all of you to pray. Pray for a world that will not accept the sign of this joy: My Mother and yours. I send her to you with compassion and love, to share with all God's children.

The Prophets preached with power and strength before I came with humility and love. My Mother, she preaches with humility and love and precedes My coming with power and strength.

It is so important for the world to understand that to call Me brother, the Mother must be accepted. I deem that through My Mother, those souls that come to her loving embrace will be able to see the signs—the signs of the times. Pray for those who reject My Mother and still shout, "Lord! Lord!"

Tomorrow is her feast day,[82] that beautiful feast that commemorates the uniting of a sinless soul, a soul without spot or stain, to a human form, as *God's most perfect creation*. Rejoice, and do as I command: bring My Mother into your homes. Love her as your true Mother. Love her as My Mother. Love her as I love her. She is truly the gate to My Heart, and she offers, freely, entrance to all.

Be at peace, My children, for I shower you with My mercy.

---

[82] The Feast of the Immaculate Conception

MESSAGE FROM MARY
DECEMBER 14, 1994

My beautiful children, it is I, your loving Mother who speaks with you this day. Again, I thank you for all your prayers and supplications, and I ask that you renew, with vigor, your devotion to the Sacred Heart . . . renounce Satan . . . and practice mortifications.

These fastings, these sacrifices, are necessary, my children, because they help to win souls, cast out demons, and strengthen you in virtue. Our Lord asks no sacrifice of you that is unnecessary or not helpful. If your vision was perfectly clear, you would be repelled from those things that you are asked to sacrifice. These things are mostly events, activities, practices, or habits that lead one to devotion of self, rather than their Creator. With grace, your heart will discern the difference because you are not called to be unhappy or mournful. If you ask me, I will help you with this mortification, in both discernment and practice.

Be joyful, humble, and above all, obedient. Have faith and confidence in me and my plan, for I assure you, victory is close. Even now, angels of truth assemble my cohort. The march on Satan's citadel is at hand. Know that I am with you all. Have confidence and believe, my children. I leave you now with my blessing. Good-bye.

MESSAGE FROM MARY
DECEMBER 21, 1994

My dear children, it is I, your Mother, who speaks with you, and I thank you for assembling in this cenacle of prayer, and I thank you for preparing your hearts to celebrate the coming of my Son and Our Lord.[83]

What a beautiful babe He was, cheerful of disposition— the completeness of joy and love. Oh, my children, how I love Him so! There was no pain, only the ecstasy of the knowledge of the nearness of God, the God to Whom I gave all that I have and was, in consecration for His holy work. What great things He has truly done for me.[84]

My children, my Son, the Lord of Lords, wishes to speak with you now. Please bow your heads and open your hearts.

MESSAGE FROM JESUS

My children, be at peace this Christmas. Enjoy the closeness of My Sacred Heart to all of you. I come this day to share with you a great truth, a truth about My Mother, who suffered so much.

She repaired the damage caused by Eve in such a way that God exalted her above all creation. I tell you, God loves her dearly for her sacrifice. All good mothers love their children, and to see them suffer, to see them in pain, is an agony. I tell you, she bore every stripe, and every step I took, and every agony I felt, on her heart. Oh, the suffering that Immaculate and sinless heart endured . . . the crucible of

---

[83] The coming of Christmas
[84] Luke 1:49: The Magnificat

suffering so intense, that no creature that ever was or ever will be, will see its equal.

And it was a threefold suffering: the suffering of a mother seeing her child tortured, imprisoned, blasphemed; the suffering of seeing the siblings causing the suffering; and finally, to endure and observe deicide.[85] The spiritual pain that she shared in was immeasurable . . . and she shared this with me. For this gift of love to all of you, she has been made Queen of Heaven. And I ask all of you to share in this love through devotion to her and her loving and Immaculate Heart. I love you all, and I leave you with my Christmas blessing.

Good-bye.

---

[85] **Deicide:** the act of killing a divine being

MESSAGE FROM MARY
DECEMBER 28, 1994

My children, it is I, your Mother, who speaks with you this day. Here we are together in this cenacle of prayer, and I hold you as I held my Son, these days after His birth so long ago. Even as an infant, He was perfect in His interior life . . . the life of the soul. And it is to this that all of you are called. It is to this that I ask a commitment of you to follow me.

I have told you that I will speak to your hearts—and this is so true, my children. But you must be prepared. This preparation consists of practicing virtue, prayer, fasting, and mortifications, and receipt of the Sacraments. The Sacraments cleanse you, my children, for your failings and sins is the mud that stuffs the ears of the soul, the dirt that blinds the eyes.

What is this "speaking" that I tell you of? At times, it's an awareness of my presence, a sense of direction, a fearlessness in the work of God. Don't be anxious about this, my children. Please be patient and understand that the Lord works in His time. All of you are special and so very different. Do not compare yourselves. Be at peace and allow God's hand to mold you into the perfect children you were meant to be.

I leave you now with my love and blessings. Good-bye.

MESSAGE FROM MARY
JANUARY 4, 1995

My beautiful children, it is I, your Mother, who speaks with you this day, and I thank you for your gracious giving. I also thank you for your attendance in my cenacle of prayer in weather that is so bad.[86]

My children, I have tried to teach you about the necessity of prayer, fasting and mortifications, receipt of the Sacraments, and the practice of virtues. And I have tried to teach you for one purpose alone, to bring you closer to my Son. This is done because your interior life is made perfect, and you are then better able to discern God's will for you. Lacking any of these elements that I have talked of, you run the danger of groping in blindness for the answers you seek.

I say this not to frighten you, my children, but to console you. Determining God's will, at times, can be very difficult. You are usually left with nothing but faith and hope. My children, I know how this is. If you study my life, you will know this to be true. One caution I give you: be patient with yourselves. Allow God to reward you with successes. You must temper your pursuit.

Good-bye, my children. I love you all, and I leave you with my Son's abundant blessings and the great gift of mercy.

---

[86] The weather was severe wind and rain.

MESSAGE FROM MARY
JANUARY 11, 1995

Oh, My beautiful children, it is I, your Mother, who speaks with you this day. I love you so, and I thank you for your beautiful prayers. You prayed the Rosary today as one, in my Son, Jesus. You are learning well, my children.

Today I come to speak of love, a love that is greater than all loves. I speak of the love that allows the sacrifice of oneself for the beloved. This can be a martyrdom of quick and persecuted death. But it is also the little sacrifices, those little things you leave behind or return to the Father with such graciousness. I call you all to be meek and humble. Recognize your sinful natures, but do not despair, for my Son's mercy is boundless, and He is always ready to shower you with His blessings.

You are called to love your family of humanity, and you do this by desiring the greater good for them . . . each and every one. I repeat that *no greater love does a man have than to offer his life for his beloved.*[87] Offer this daily by renouncing yourselves. When you fall, pray for God's grace, stand again, and continue on. Depend upon the Communion of Saints— the whole Church, whose prayers unite to ask of God His benevolence. On this day, a soul prays for you.[88] Please pray for all the souls of the departed . . . in one faith . . . in the love of my Son.

Peace to all of you, my children, and I offer you my blessings as I say good-bye.

---

[87] John 15:13

[88] Earlier this day, the funeral Mass and burial took place for one of our cenacle members, Lydia, who died of cancer. Our Blessed Mother may be referring to this person, when she says: "On this day a soul prays for you."

MESSAGE FROM MARY
JANUARY 18, 1995

My beautiful children, it is I, your Mother, who speaks with you this day. I am truly in your presence, and I ask that you gather round so that I may comfort you and explain to you the necessity for your crosses.

My beautiful loved ones, it is through your crosses that sanctity is reached. I affirm that it is the only and true path to holiness. I know it's hard to see this now, but the crosses of life are great gifts from the Father, for it is on the cross, and only on the cross, that you can truly give completely of yourselves.

On the cross, there is no hidden motivation, no selfish benefit, only suffering sweetly given to the Lord of Lords. In this offering is love. In this offering is an acceptance of the Father's will. And the love you give is magnified beyond comprehension, for you become one with the ocean of my Son's charity. And all of this is contained in the cross.

Rejoice, and bear up as best you can—and know that if you are united with me in prayer, the burden will never be too much. You will always have the strength, and your final destination will be assured.

Be at peace now, my children. Quiet your hearts. Allow my words to enter you and bring you closer to my Immaculate Heart.

Good-bye.

MESSAGE FROM MARY
JANUARY 25, 1995

My beautiful children, it is I, your Mother, the Mother of your Lord, who speaks with you this day. I thank you for your prayers and your attentive concern for my holy intentions.

My children, you truly live in the times of the great apostasy,[89] that time foretold, when so many of God's children would abandon Truth and run from the Light. This is evident everywhere. So many of my children remain obstinate and full of self-will, and they spread throughout the sheepfold, full of lies and distortion.

Remain steadfast, my children. Stay with the doctrines handed on to you from the apostles—those doctrines preserved by my Son's Church and His Vicar.[90] Be resolute and have faith that the victory of my Immaculate Heart is near. The numbers in my humble cohort are swelling. So many souls are being called back to the Faith by the power of the Holy Spirit. So rejoice. The light of dawn is approaching.

Be at peace, my children, but continue your fervent prayers for my intentions. Ask for all in my Son's name, and it will be given. Allow your conscience to be developed and formed in my Immaculate Heart. Allow the Spirit to do His work. Be at peace now, my children, and know that I pray for you a prayer that never ceases. Good-bye.

---

[89] **Apostasy:** renunciation of the Faith; abandonment of a previous loyalty: defection

[90] Message given during the pontificate of Pope John Paul II

MESSAGE FROM MARY
FEBRUARY 1, 1995

My beautiful children, it is I, your loving Mother who is with you this day. Your prayers and devotions are so appreciated, and their value is immeasurable. Continue, be persistent, for they lead to your edification.

My children, humility and obedience are the virtues you must develop if you are to come closer to my Son. Pride and rebellion are the seeds of destruction. They led to man's fall from grace, and they distort faith. This great gift from God is twisted and contorted into a religion of practice, and this practice is always conformed to man's will. It shades and clouds the truth and makes it impossible to know, love, and serve God as you were meant to. This is why my Son exclaimed in joy that in God's mercy, the light is revealed to the little, the humble, and the gentle.

My children, my dear children, please practice these virtues. Know that I will help you. In this way your hearts will be conformed to mine, and I will comfort you as we approach the threshold of honor and glory, which is at the feet of my Son.

Good-bye, my little ones. I leave you with my blessing of love and peace.

MESSAGE FROM MARY
FEBRUARY 8, 1995

My beautiful and loving children, it is I, your Mother, and I have come this day to speak with you and be near you. I love you all so much, and I thank you for your prayers.

As you advance in holiness, this prayer of yours becomes more and more beautiful. I gather them as roses in a beautiful bouquet, and heaven is filled with their beauty. Holiness, my children, is where I wish to lead you to. And a very important thing to always keep foremost in your attentions is the virtue of humility. Always pray for the grace of humility, that the Father may shower you with it because humility and holiness are so closely linked. In fact, one cannot be present without the other.

Humility is not a weakness of spirit or a lack of strength. It is rather, an open heart that truly sees and responds to reality. This barrier, this inability to see oneself, slows the progress of so many of my children. Pray for this virtue without ceasing, and it will be given to you. At times you fall, you give in to pride, or the other enemies of this virtue. I know this is true. But please understand this, that each time you pick yourself up, recognize your mistakes, and ask forgiveness, your soul is exalted . . . and love for you increases, as love increases in you.

I assure you I am very near to each of your hearts. I am always here to bless and console you and will remain always your Mother. Let my peace fill you. I bathe you in the warmth of my Son's graces. Good-bye, my children. Be at peace.

MESSAGE FROM MARY
FEBRUARY 15, 1995

Beautiful children of God, it is I, your Mother, the Mother of your Lord, who speaks with you this day.

My children, I assure you, you will be lights to the world. Great "hosannas" will be raised at the glimpse of my Son, and this glimpse they will see in you, as you grow in perfection and increase in love. I know and understand your pain and suffering with regards to the direction of the world. I am here, my children, to comfort you, as I comforted and supported the apostles before they received the Spirit.

Beware the leaven of the world! This leaven is a worldly way of thinking—human-centered and selfish by its very nature. Its veneer of love and concern is very thin and always ends in anguish and disappointment. To understand the effects of this leaven, think of bread that is molded and shaped in the baker's hands. He creates it for a purpose. But for that bread to maintain its shape, its purpose, it must be unleavened. For with yeast, it follows its own will and changes in shape and use, different from that intended by the baker. You, my children, are unleavened bread, shaped and molded for a purpose, a purpose truly understood only by God.

There is much for you to do to prepare for my Son's Kingdom. For now, find contentment in your prayer and your existence *in* the world, without being *of* the world. Good-bye, my children. I leave you with my peace and the hope that it will fill your hearts.

MESSAGE FROM MARY
FEBRUARY 22, 1995

My children, it is I, your Mother, who speaks with you, and I wish to fill your hearts with joy.

Please know that I am with you throughout your day. I am never far from your side. I am always ready to help if you stumble. Please invoke my name at times of stress and temptation. I am the Mother that is always ready to help her children. I am ever vigilant and will never abandon you.

I have told you many times to beware of Satan's darkness—the storm clouds of his dissention and arrogance. I tell you this so that you may see it and discern it; but do not fear it. Fear only the Father, for Satan's darkness, that blackness that envelopes the earth, is illusion. It is not real because it will be destroyed by the light of my Son, the growing light of salvation that will cover and illumine all.

It is with dispensation from God, under His authority and with His grace, that I come to you in this way, and I will continue until your hearts have been prepared and understand fully the mission that my Son has laid out for each of you. Rest secure in this, and know that I love you all.

Good-bye, my loving children. Peace be with all of you.

MESSAGE FROM MARY
MARCH 1, 1995

Beautiful children of God, it is I, the Mother of the Suffering One, who is with you this day. I thank you so much for your beautiful Rosary. The power of this prayer is beyond description. I tell you, when you pray thus, you storm the gates of heaven. My Son will never refuse them.

During this Lenten season, my children, I ask you to meditate on Reconciliation—its necessity and its meaning. For in Reconciliation you find the desire of your heart, by uniting your will more perfectly with the Father's. This *is* holiness, my children . . . the unity of wills. And you do this by obeying His commandments and following the wise counsels of His Church.

To be perfected in holiness, your hearts must be prepared by the practice of virtue to discern God's divine providence. And further, you must become detached from all your possessions. Detachment is so important, my children, for there lies perfection. My Son told the rich man to give away all that he had to become perfect. Many make the mistake, oftentimes, of taking this in the literal sense only. It means to be detached, as your station in life allows, and in this way, conform yourself to His Spirit.

To prepare for Reconciliation, my children, cast your gaze upon the Crucified One. Look into His eyes, and see that He loves you and forgives you. Ask Him to bare your souls, and remember His words: "God, forgive them, they know not what they do."[91] With such a favor and such love, you can do nothing but rejoice. My Son, the Savior, loves you so. Be afraid of nothing.

Good-bye, my children.

---

[91] Luke 23:34

MESSAGE FROM MARY
MARCH 3, 1995

My beautiful children, it is I, your Mother, and the Mother of your Lord, who is with you now. The peace and serenity that you offer to my Immaculate Heart is a beautiful gift, a gift that will not go unrewarded.

I am always with you, my children, and I am, in a special way, always with you because you have offered me your hearts. Only those hearts offered to me with love and humility can be cleansed by the special graces that my Son offers in these times. I am always ready to prepare a heart that is offered to me to be presented to my Son.

He loves you so, my children. One loving glance at a crucifix will fill your heart with this fact. His feet are transfixed on the path to God. He leads all just souls there. His hands are attached firmly, in pain and suffering, to all of humanity. In this way He guides you, helps you, and if need be, carries you, to that home in heaven that awaits you all. You need only ask, my children.

During these times, the enemy of love, the enemy of life, will burden you deeply with his temptations and his accusations. Hold steadfast, my children. You are worthy of your destiny. To deny this is to denigrate the value of my Son's supreme Sacrifice, for it is in this that you are made worthy. It is in this that I am made worthy.

I now fill your hearts with my Son's peace and love. Know that I am so close, so very close to all of your hearts. Good-bye, my children.

MESSAGE FROM MARY
MARCH 8, 1995

My loving children, it is I, your Mother, the Mother of Mercy and of Divine Strength, who speaks with you this day. I come to gather you all under the protection of my Immaculate Heart. Those of my children who remain there in spirit are always protected. All the wiles of the enemy will not prevail if you do this, my children.

At this time, Satan is intensifying his efforts to dissuade, to confuse and frustrate those who follow my simple and humble way. He attacks faith with confusion and hopelessness. Be wary, my children. Look with your hearts to divine providence[92] to show you the way. Be most careful, at this time, of willful decisions. It is so easy to be pushed into despair or spiritual pride, without dependence on this providence.

I love you all so much, and I desire that you unite your hearts with mine in a special prayer to my Son and Our Lord:

> Grace and strength we ask of you, God,
> for all these children,
> that they remain one with Your will,
> always at the service of love
> and with unity of purpose.
> All glory, honor, and praise
> to the Trinity Most Holy.

Thanks be to the Father, and the Son, and the Holy Spirit.

Praise be the Holy Name of Jesus, my Son.

---

[92] **Providence:** divine guidance or care; God conceived as the power sustaining and guiding human destiny.

Calm your hearts, my children. *Stay with me, for I show the way to paradise.* Good-bye.

MESSAGE FROM MARY
MARCH 15, 1995

My beautiful children, it is I, the Mother of the Good Shepherd, who speaks with you this day. I thank you for your constancy in prayer, and in particular, your attendance at my cenacle. This cenacle was formed by me to prepare you. And for what is to come, my children, you need this preparation so desperately.

This is the time of the enemy . . . this is his season. He is a wolf among the sheep; and you, my children, are my lost little lambs, brought back to me by a gift of grace, so that I may protect you in the folds of my mantle. Let me feed you and strengthen you with the Mother's milk of redemption and truth. Accept my love. Do not turn away with feelings of unworthiness. These are temptations and accusations from the "ugly one."

My children, I know you desire to test your strength because you become healthy. You wish to be loose to prance about the sheepfold. My children, fight this urge. Remain close to my heart, for there is much preparation left to do. Find time in the busyness of your lives to pray with me—a quiet time when you can speak to me from your hearts and share with me your innermost secrets and desires.

When you do this, know that I am always with you. This promise I have made to you many times, and a Mother always keeps her promises. The more you do this, my children, the keener will become your awareness of my presence and of the divine life that lives within you. Be moderate. Do this at times allowed by your station in life. But be consistent, as is your attendance at this cenacle.

I love you all so much, and I long for the day when I can present you to my Son as spotless and beautiful lambs, groomed in His image. Be at peace now, my children. Find solace and contentment in this message. In my heart is your shelter, now and always.

Good-bye, my children.

MESSAGE FROM MARY
MARCH 22, 1995

My beautiful children, it is I, your loving Mother, and the Mother of your Lord, who speaks with you this day. Remain in the peace that God offers you. Remain firm and resolute if you find yourself in the desert. Know at these times I am very close to you.

The Spirit of Consolation is fleeting. He comes when you need Him, and at times, He comes in reward. Do not pursue Him, my children. You must learn to find comfort in your prayer at times of dryness, for this is the period of growth, the time when you are strengthened. As my Son approached His glory, the Spirit was completely withdrawn. Should you be different, my children?

By the grace of God, you have been given the eyes to see and the hearts to feel the pain and anguish of a Mother as her Son is dying. You see this in the torment of my Son's Church, the Church that God has given me to protect and to nurture in these times. I am the true Ark that protects God's children.

I urge all of you to come unto me. Remain close and protected from the vile waters of sin and hatred that is drowning so many of my children. This attack is gathering strength and will soon become so strong that only those souls protected in the refuge of my Immaculate Heart can avoid the severest damage to their souls. This does not mean, my children, that you are to be without hope, for I tell you, the Light of Dawn, my glorious Son, shall shine from all your hearts and be made available to so many who hang on—by the tender threads—to love and salvation.

Continue in your prayers. The time of preparation continues. Let nothing deter you on your path to holiness. I love you all so much, my children, and I share this love equally with all of you. This day, I increase my prayers for each of you that you remain strong and united. Good-bye, my children.

MESSAGE FROM MARY
APRIL 5, 1995

My beautiful and loving children, it is I, your Mother, and the Mother of your Lord, who speaks with you this day. My children, I love you so, and I thank you for your prayers. They are the true arms with which the battle is fought . . . and this battle is so important for so many souls. Your love of God grows deeper, my children; and as time continues, it will get deeper still, provided you persevere in three most important areas:

- First, you must be constant in denying yourselves little things or big things, depending upon your capacity. But it is so important that you are consistent.
- Second, you must pray. Pray at those times allowed by your duties, in a formal way. Have your hearts in the presence of God at all times. Make your lives a living prayer.
- Third, receive the Sacraments as often as is practical.

If you do these things, my children, you will win against all obstacles. No matter the challenge against faith or hope or love, you will overcome. I promise you the grace will always be there. You need only respond.

To the world, my Son is the "King of Thorns." His Kingdom is a cross of pain, torture, and humiliation so deep. His drink is bitter gall. His food is the wretched herbs and weeds that grow where they will. But to us, my children . . . to us, He is the Summation of Love, the ultimate offering of sacrifice to appease the justice of God—enough to save a thousand worlds! Pray, my children, that your brothers and sisters will not refuse these great graces.

At this time, I *implore* that you avoid confrontation. I know the desire to defend is so very strong, to strike out, to lash back. *Please* be quiet and humble. I do not mean by this to be silent or cowardly when confronting the suffering of my Son. Rather, be like the young woman who tenderly and lovingly cleansed His face as He made His way to the hill of pain. In this way, show your courage, my children. Comfort my Church. Pray for my Son's priests. Let your devotions be seen. Remain steadfast.

My Son will not desert you or leave you in your pain and your sufferings. When He finds you lying on the road in pain and anguish, He cleanses you and anoints you with healing oil. My children, even at this, He does not finish. He returns as often as required to meet your needs.[93] Be at peace. Know that I love you and will always be with you. Good-bye.

---

[93] During the message, Walter was shown internally and made to understand that the story of the Good Samaritan is actually an explanation of how Jesus cares for each of us. When He finds us wounded and in need, He picks us up, cleanses our wounds with water and dresses them with oil, and places us in the care of the Church, which ministers to us. To the innkeeper, who represents God the Father, He makes a payment—His sacrifice on the Cross—and promises to return to make any further payment necessary. The story of the Good Samaritan seems to portray the spiritual need we have when we are wounded by sin. Jesus comes to us and makes atonement (payment) to the Father; He brings us to the Church to care for and heal us through the water and oil of the Sacraments; and He promises to continue to return to us in the Eucharist, which is both the perpetual offering of Himself to God for the forgiveness of our sins and food for our spiritual nourishment.

MESSAGE FROM MARY
April 12, 1995

Beautiful children of God, it is truly your heavenly Mother who speaks with you this day. Please be attentive to my words, for they lead you to holiness and ultimate joy.

What is this holiness? Where is it? Holiness is a person, and that person is my Son. He is holy because He is united to the Father's will, perfectly. It is this unity to which I direct you, my children. As you grow in strength, your vision improves, your discernment increases, and you become truly one with His will. Only in this way does anyone become holy. And like all things of value, effort is required. This is the pearl that having been found, all else is forsaken.

Soon, my Son commences His Passion: the suffering and death He endured for all of you . . . and for each of you. Envelop yourself in this mystery. Open your hearts to the graces that will flow this week, so as to be prepared for the glory and love that will burst forth so very soon.[94]

I leave you now, my children, with my peace. Remain in this quiet prayer for a few moments. In this way, it comes to rest *in* you and will surely reside the rest of this day.

---

[94] This message preceded Good Friday, Holy Saturday, and Easter Sunday—the Triduum.

MESSAGE FROM MARY
APRIL 19, 1995

My beautiful children, it is I, the Mother of the Most High, who speaks with you this day. I offer you my love, as always, and the inner consolation, provided by the Spirit for your strengthening during these times of trial.

My children, your souls are beautiful flowers of love, and they are nourished by heaven, by the Sacraments, and through your prayers at this cenacle. Your strength to endure will always be heaven-sent, regardless of the challenge, of the change, or the loss you may endure. Remember always that I am your Mother.

Remember, my children, the enemy is most active at this time. You are all of special interest to him because of the damage you cause to his plans. The world does not recognize the value of prayer, but I assure you, Satan does. And he will do all he can to dissuade you from this effort.

Many changes are afoot, and they are direct attacks at the priesthood, my Son's presence in the Eucharist, and myself. They will never convince you, my children. These attacks are not meant to. Rather, they are meant for the many souls that wander in the darkness of uncertainty. It is for these that you must pray, for these that you must witness.

I implore you, let the light that my Son fills you with shine before all men. You do this most of all through exhibiting holy and loving charity, even to those who attack you. Be at peace, my children. Go and spread my Son's love.

MESSAGE FROM MARY
APRIL 26, 1995

My loving children, it is I, your Mother, who speaks with you this day. I come to you as the Mother of Divine Providence, and in this providence you must have total faith and trust. Discernment and acceptance of God's plan for you is the true sign of holiness. Every blessing, every trial, every victory, every defeat, is a gift from God to bring you in union with Him, in total love and abandonment.

Oh, my children, no one knows the depths of His majestic works. His ways are mysterious, but the motivation is love. This is the source, the beginning and the end of all that you live through, all that you experience, and all that you must do.

The enemy is so subtle, my children, and his minions bring on persecution and defamation. My Son, in His body, was falsely accused in the beginning, and it will be in the end. Pray for those who persecute. Pray for those that will be seduced by the "new christ." Many, so many souls, will persecute in the defense of the church they believe they love.

Be at peace, my children, and have strength in the knowledge that I will always be with you. The Spirit will fill you, and you will be protected beneath my mantle, in the Ark of the True Covenant, the Ark that will flow safely over the waters of despair and trial. I leave you now, my children, with a blessing, a kiss from the Spirit, and a touch of my joy.

MESSAGE FROM MARY
MAY 3, 1995

Oh, my beautiful children, I have come again to speak with you this day, to thank you for your beautiful prayers.

It is so important, my children, that you enter into the quiet of that special room in your hearts, and invoke my Son's name in prayer. Do this especially before each cenacle because in this way, my peace can fill you and provide protection from the agitation and the anguish that the enemy throws at you so violently. *Quiet and preparation is an important secret to deep prayer, my children.*

In these times of distress, turmoil, and dissention, remember that my Son is who He claims to be, and that His prayers are always answered. So long ago, He prayed in the flesh that He and all God's children be "one in the Father."[95] This prayer continues to this day and will be answered. Unity is from my Son. Dissention and strife come from the enemy of us all. Always bear this in mind, my children, when you discern.

I love you all so much, and I ask that you continue your prayers for my special sons, my priests who are so vilified, tempted, and accused. It is a sword in my heart—the painful dagger that widens the wounds of a Mother. Console me, my children. Console me with your prayers and your loving attention.

Good-bye, my children. I leave you now with my peace that you will always find if you look inward for that special place in your heart.

---

[95] John 17:11, 21

MESSAGE FROM MARY
MAY 10, 1995

My beautiful children, it is your Mother, and the Mother of Jesus, the Word Incarnate, who speaks with you this day. His word is Truth, and His word is Life, and it is to this Life that I lead you.

I ask that you offer me your hearts. Release them from your worldly concerns. Hand them to me willingly, as a loving and tearful child bares its wounds to its mother. My charism is healing and transmitting my Son's love to all His children. No matter the times, no matter the elements, or the situations you may find yourself in, always have confidence and remain strong in hope because my Son is the Good Shepherd, and none who are written in the Book of Life shall be lost. This is why so many miracles of conversion take place, to be signs to a world gone astray, where love for brother goes cold, and even existence is questioned. The glories that await my children who persevere are so beautiful, so filling.

Let me touch your hearts in a special blessing, as I share a Mother's tears for consolation. Rest your spirits, my children. Stay close with me for a moment before I leave you with my peace and blessing. Good-bye.

MESSAGE FROM JESUS
MAY 24, 1995

Greetings, children of God and children of Mary. I come this day to share with you a great truth and to ask of you something important.

My Mother is first in heaven, not because of her nature, but because of her virtue. Her love is an offer to *all* of God's children to reach the heights of My presence. It is through her that I come to you . . . and you come to Me. It has been deemed thus from the beginning of time. The Spirit truly overshadows her. Through her, all are born anew. Her hand is offered to all. Pray for those who refuse, for her hand is only offered in the hope that you will take it and come to Me.

It is through the power of her intercession, combined with the prayers of the saints, that the water of this world will be converted to wine by the Holy Spirit. She has asked, and I will do it.[96] So in preparation for this great indwelling, I ask you all to live your consecrations in peace and humble docility to My Vicar,[97] who needs your prayers and support so desperately in these times. Have hope . . . for I am coming.

I leave you now with My peace and My blessing. Good-bye.

---

[96] John 2:3
[97] Message given during the pontificate of Pope John Paul II

MESSAGE FROM MARY
MAY 31, 1995

My children, it is I, your Mother, who speaks with you this day. I thank you for your prayers, your humble submission to God's will, and joining together your hearts and minds in my cenacle of prayer. This is especially pleasing to me on my feast day,[98] my children, and again, I thank you. The world is in such need of prayer.

I am in your midst this day with the Infant Lord, my beautiful Child of Eternity. I bring Him to you, as I bring Him to all God's children. This mission I have been given from eternity, and in this I am so blest. He loves you all so much, and you are asked to imitate Him. Imitate His purity, His gentleness, His innocence.

Be not afraid of your devotions, of your love for Him, and your love for His humble servant.[99] He is my Child and my Lord, and I wish so much to share Him freely with all of God's children. This is why I bring Him to you, to prepare you as His cousin John was prepared so long ago. Your brightness will make paths straight[100] for so many souls. Through you they will see the way . . . dimly at first, but gradually gathering in brightness and intensity. They will follow, children; I ask you to set the example.

Continue in your prayers. Pursue your duties with vigor and joy. Know that in addition to offering Him, I offer you my maternal assistance. I am willing to work by your side at the most meager of chores.[101] I love you all so much, and I ask that

---

[98] Feast of the Visitation

[99] His humble servant: Our Lady speaks of herself, the "handmaid of the Lord."

[100] St. John the Baptist cried, ". . . prepare ye the way of the Lord, make straight His paths." (Luke 3:4)

[101] Our Blessed Mother offers her assistance in the same way she assisted her cousin Elizabeth.

you keep this message in your heart, and spread my devotion. Good-bye, my children.

MESSAGE FROM MARY
JUNE 7, 1995

My beautiful children, it is I, your Mother, who speaks with you this day. I bring you heaven's blessings and the consolation of rest in my arms. Be at peace, my children. Find joy in my maternal compassion.

I tell you, these times of the cenacle are times of healing and rejuvenation. Even now, my servant Raphael anoints you with my special ointment, the healing salve to quiet souls in pain and sorrow. Pray for heavenly strength and endurance, for human strength and endurance is incapable of bearing the Cross of my Son. It is in helping my Son bear the Cross of redemption that the Father loves you so, for in no other way does the Father hear the Son's voice through your pleadings and groanings.

My children, I love you so, and I thank you for your participation in the "great intercession" that will bring about the flood of God's mercy upon all your brothers and sisters. I promise you, my children, a time when pain will be no more. All will be light. All will be love. Words cannot describe this, so you are given the gift of the Spirit to know this truth in your hearts. The enemy will try to cloud, will try to hide this, and at times, his work will seem oppressive. But through my gift, in your heart of hearts, in the darkest times, you will know this vision resides in you.

Go now, my children. *Let joy be your witness to confound the world.* Good-bye.

MESSAGE FROM MARY
JUNE 14, 1995

My beautiful little ones, it is your heavenly Mother who speaks with you this day.

You are part of my assembly, my assembly of little and humble soldiers who will carry my Son's banner of light throughout the world. You are most courageous, my children, in your prayers and in the dutiful living of your vocations. In this way, you reflect the light of my Son in a most effective manner.

Let me mold you and shape you. Continue to have recourse to me for all your needs. In these times the waters of darkness spread, and the only true refuge is my Immaculate Heart. Reside there, my children, in the true haven of blessed souls. It is the Ark that will carry you over the waters of destruction. Your passage there is humble service to my Son's law of love, and in this Ark reside the true ministers, the true kings, and the true prophets.

Humility is the key, my children. Be at peace with your brothers and sisters in the one Lord. Obey His Vicar[102] in all things. Continue to pray and offer up those little sacrifices. I love you all so much, my children, and your part in my great mission is manifesting itself even this day. Let peace reign in your hearts. Accept my gifts, and remain always close. Good-bye, my children. . . . Good-bye.

---

[102] Message given during the pontificate of Pope John Paul II

MESSAGE FROM MARY
JUNE 21, 1995

My beautiful and loving children, it is I, your Mother, who gathers with you at the foot of my Son's Cross to offer Him our sorrows and our joys and the pain of the sword that wounds our souls. This is a great gift that heaven has allowed me to share with you: to participate in a Mother's suffering, and so be prepared to know *such* joy.

Do not look at the Cross with fear, my children . . . nor should you look at it with self-doubt. Be at peace because the Lord of Lords knows your littleness, your inabilities, your abject weakness. This is what makes His love so great—that He gave His life for you so that you may have life.

The Cross is a gateway for mercies and graces, and the key to this gateway are the crosses you bear yourselves. Carry them humbly, joyfully, and with the strength that God gives you. I implore you, do not reject your crosses, for they lead you to my Son. I implore that you join my procession of crosses, large and small, because this procession is led by myself to the light that will fill all who accept my lead.

Be at peace, my children. Help to redeem those that reject the Truth. *Time is so short, and for many, it may be too late.* Pray fervently, especially for priests. Your local church is under my special protection, but I need your prayers, my children. The enemy attacks from many sides.

I love you all, and I leave you with my maternal blessing. Please know that I hold you all close to my heart and that I protect you always. Good-bye.

MESSAGE FROM MARY
JUNE 28, 1995

My beautiful and loving children, it is your Mother[103] who speaks with you now.

Jesus is one with the Father and one with the Holy Spirit. He is one with Them in the unity of the divine nature, and I am His Mother. Closely aligned with this mystery is the source of your very being and purpose. You are called to be God's children. You are Jesus' brothers and sisters, and you are called to be one with God for all eternity.

To achieve this goal, my children, you must respond to the grace of heaven with loving and contrite spirits. The way of perfection is a rocky road, full of pitfalls and delays. This is why my Son has ordained that I be your benefactress[104] in heaven, to guide you and bring you to Him. Only in perfection may you participate in the life of God because He *is* perfection; and to be one with Him, no imperfection may remain.

Self-will is the enemy that corrodes your beautiful and humble attempts at this perfection. Let go of self, and allow my Son to live in you . . . and live for you. When temptations or life's choices come your way, ask not, "What should I do?" Ask, "What would Jesus do?" And then do what your heart tells you to do, because if you have given your heart to Jesus, it is one with Him. And then, you obey Him.

I love you all so much, and my life is a continuous prayer for my children . . . for each of you. I leave you now with a Mother's blessing. Good-bye.

---

[103] Our Lady is showing us that she is truly the Mother of God, and also our Mother.

[104] **Benefactress:** one that confers a benefit, especially one that makes a gift or bequest.

MESSAGE FROM MARY
JULY 12, 1995

My beautiful children, how happy I am that you are all together this day in my cenacle. My children, this is a great fruit that I offer to my Son—formed and molded in my hands, prepared for the action of the Holy Spirit, and endowed with the strength of my Son's Sacrifice. It was the will of the Father that you be formed in this way. And the process continues, my children.

Always prepare yourselves for the Holy Mass in a worthy manner. Be recollected and at peace with your brother. Only in this way can you enter into the Sacrifice, that great mystery that sealed the fruits of Adam's fault and allows you to become one with the Father. You are destined to be children of God and to be one with Him, as my Son is one with Him.

When my Son is elevated, look upon Him. Enter into the mystery of Calvary, the glorious Sacrifice, acceptable to the Father, that paid the price for your *true* freedom. Remember that it is at this time, you unite with the angels and saints in heaven in giving praise and honor and glory to the Most Holy Trinity—God without beginning or end, Creator of all, Benevolent Love—that fills your very being, if you turn to Him. Be at peace, my children. The peace that comes from this unity is yours, if you ask and receive.

I leave you all with my Maternal blessings and my Mother's love. Good-bye.

MESSAGE FROM MARY
JULY 19, 1995

My beautiful children, this day I ask you to consider your Mother's Immaculate Heart, for it is an ocean of love and the fountain of my Son's mercies. I wish you all to share in the delivery of these saving graces. Be conduits, my children, of this inexhaustible source. As large as it is, it is but a drop in comparison to my Heavenly Son's. It is through Him that all love and salvation is open to all of you. I am filled with love; but He *is* love.

To advance in holiness and be these conduits, my children, you must abandon yourselves to the Lord of Lords. Hold nothing back. Give Him everything. If you leave nothing for yourself, I promise you will be filled . . . and filled with much greater things. *You will become my Son.* He will fill your hearts, and then the light will shine, the light so desperately needed at this time.

Remember, my children, always, that this light must bear the wood of the cross. There is no other way. I know at times this is very difficult, but I have promised, and I continue to promise to all of you my assistance and a share of my Maternal strength and dignity. So be at peace, for with every burden will come some rest and great consolation.

Pray for hope to fight despair, love to fight hatred, and holy faith to defeat doubt and delusion. Good-bye, my children. I love you all so much, and I leave you now with my special blessing.

MESSAGE FROM MARY
JULY 26, 1995

My beautiful children, it is I, your Mother, who speaks with you this day, and I thank you for your beautiful prayers and your tender offerings. They will be put to a great use—the use of tremendous value for my work.

I prepare you as part of my work, to be lights to a darkened world, to share my Son's love and hope. In this way you will draw all men to the Father. My children, please understand this. It is far better to show Jesus than to describe Him. I promise—if you remain diligent—to clarify[105] your earthen vessels so all may be illuminated.

The words I speak to you are true, because I bring you to Truth, Himself, and my witness who testifies on my behalf is my Spouse, through Whose power all is accomplished. See the events unfold as a witness, my children. Feel the touching of your hearts and the things you are shown and given, as signs of the Holy Spirit to verify the truth of my words and my work.

Be at peace and have courage. Know that He[106] is with you always, with my Son and the Father, behind me in every effort in prayer I offer on your behalf. Work through Him, in Him, and with Him in all things.

Be at peace, my children. I bless you all. Good-bye.

---

[105] **Clarify:** to make clear or understandable; to free from impurities; to become clear or transparent. Synonym: purify, to free from sin or defilement
[106] The Holy Spirit

MESSAGE FROM MARY
AUGUST 2, 1995

My beautiful children, it is I, your Mother, who speaks with you now. Be at peace. Remain in hope, for you are diamonds, shined and prepared in my maternal hands.

Know that heaven awaits your work, the work inspired by my Immaculate Heart and spread by the power of the Holy Spirit. This great work will rejuvenate hearts, change minds, and save souls. And you will all play your part because as dutiful children, you've given yourselves to me. In spite of trials, sufferings, and difficulties, I promise you great joy and happiness.

Have confidence in me. Know that I am your Mother and that I guard your every step. Keep your hearts pure so that they may respond to grace. Continue in your prayers. Spend time in the presence of my Son. I have said this so many times in so many places, and yet so many of my children fail to listen. But the Lord has His time, and He has His places for each of you.

Be patient, my children. If you find no peace in your hearts, come to me, pray with me, for the Lord of consolation loves His children and will not abandon them. Oh, how He loves a resolute soul! I love you all, and I leave you with my peace and a mother's kiss for each of you. Good-bye.

MESSAGE FROM MARY
AUGUST 9, 1995

My beautiful children, it is I, your Mother, who speaks with you now. I wish to share with you my abundant joy, for soon He comes—to fill men's hearts, to show all peoples the Truth, the Way and the Life. Peace will reign, and joy will be everlasting.

Have confidence in your Mother and my Maternal plan, for your salvation, and the salvation of so many, hinges on their acceptance of my Son. Time is short, so remain fervent in your prayers. Practice humility, charity, and all the virtues. The Holy Spirit will give you the strength. You have only to hand over your wills. This I promise you.

It is my wish that you all be little saints, my children, and to do this, you have only to stay with me. Rest in my arms and allow me to share the knowledge of my Son with you, so that you in turn, may go out and share it with the world. You are part of my little army—my advancing little ones who will smash the walls of hatred, of blasphemy, and all the signs of men that offend the Father so very much.

Be at peace, my children, and remain close. I love you all so much. Good-bye.

MESSAGE FROM MARY
AUGUST 16, 1995

My beautiful children, my little prayerful ones, how holy you are becoming. Continue your prayers, your fastings and mortifications. Intensify them, if you can. In all things, look to my Son for strength and encouragement. Know that I am with you always. It is in Him, and through Him, and with Him, that all the mighty works of my plan *were being* accomplished. For those who can see, providence[107] is clearly at work. Let this give you courage and hope, for the reign of God is at hand and even now in your midst.[108] Rejoice and be joyful of spirit.

Find God in the little things, the blessings, and the opportunities to acquire treasure in heaven. These are all graces that spring from the Almighty's munificence[109] and His great love for all His children. Pray that the Spirit gives you the strength of virtue to respond, and that you remain always steadfast in the Light. I will show you the direction. I will bear the witness for you, my children. Continue to bear witness for me.

I love you all, and I leave you with my blessing and a Mother's caress. Remain at peace. Give your troubles to my Son so they may be transfixed to the Cross. Then you will be healed. Good-bye.

---

[107] **Providence:** the care exercised by God over the universe; an event or circumstances ascribable to divine interposition; God.

[108] Ref: Luke 17:20-21

[109] **Munificence:** extraordinarily generous or bountiful. (Note: the previous day was the Feast Day of the Assumption of Mary, which is defined and described by Pope Pius XII in the document with the name: *Munificentissimus Deus*.)

MESSAGE FROM MARY
AUGUST 30, 1995

My beautiful children, I come to you this day as the Mother of Hope. Allow my hope to fill you, this hope which has as its source my beautiful Son, the True Hope of all the universe. This hope is a great gift from God. It allows your clouded vision to see beyond life's turmoil and difficulties.

For so many, a lack of hope blinds them to the love and humility of God. They cannot see how God would manifest Himself in such a lowly way: born of poor parentage, living a life of labor, offering Himself in a martyrdom for the love of His fellow man. "God would not manifest Himself this way. It would be glorious and powerful." This is what they think. But I tell you my children, a God Who cherishes love and humility above all else because it is good, must be supremely humble and full of love because He *is all* good. This is the simple but mysterious answer, my children, to the Incarnation.[110]

And for those whose hearts are opened, this hope I bring will fill and fill, until there is no room for despair. All you need—all your love and all the strength for the coming battle, is provided to you in prayer and the Sacraments. Pray with me often, especially the "Our Father," my children. Ask me to come to you and pray the supreme prayer with you . . . and I will.

---

[110] **Incarnation:** The assumption of the human nature by Jesus Christ as the Second Person of the Most Holy Trinity. The act of becoming embodied in flesh. Biblical references to the love and humility of the Incarnation: "The Word became flesh" (John 1:14). The Son of God "was manifested in the flesh" (1 Tim 3:16). "Have this in mind among yourselves, which is yours in Christ Jesus, who, though he was in the form of God, did not count equality with God a thing to be grasped, but emptied himself, taking the form of a servant, being born in the likeness of men. And being found in human form, he humbled himself and became obedient unto death, even death on a cross" (Phil 2:5-8).

Have courage! Great things are about to transpire for my children—those who have been faithful, *those who endure the trial*. Be at peace. Resign your sufferings to the Cross, as a gift to my Son. If you do this, you will find Him most generous, my children. I love you all, and I leave you with my peace and a kiss of humble joy.

MESSAGE FROM MARY
SEPTEMBER 13, 1995

My beautiful children, on this beautiful day, I thank you for gathering to pray as one, on behalf of my special desires for you and for the Church. Be at peace and remain under the protection of a Mother's care. I love you all so much and will never abandon you. *Those times when the trial is most severe, I am closest.*[111] Always remember to pray with me. Ask, and you will receive my help. I never rest in this endeavor, my children, and I direct and lead and help you toward the goal that has been your destinies from the beginning.

Be not afraid. Embrace the cross. I know, at times, this is very difficult. You grumble and squirm and then heap more blame upon yourselves for your lack of grace. Do not do this, my children. Simply gaze lovingly at my Son, at the image of His Sacrifice. When no consolation is left for you, when you are as dry as the desert, engage in this practice. Look lovingly upon Him. With the assent of your will, ask, and He will give. He died so that He could fill your hearts. You only need be receptive and you will be filled with the light of eternity, the joy forever, that can be seen by all your brothers and sisters.

The end of the false prophets[112] *is at hand*, my children. Their lies and deceptions, even now, begin to burn with the fire that cleanses. Truth will prevail, in spite of intermittent darkness and despair. His victory is complete. And even the usurpers[113] and those that twist Truth work to God's grand design, for in this way, His glory is manifest to all creation. The true

---

[111] When the trial was most severe for Jesus, our Blessed Mother was closest to Him at the foot of the Cross.

[112] False prophets in the Old Testament were identified as those who led the people of God astray by telling them that everything was alright, that their behavior was acceptable to God.

[113] **Usurper:** one who seizes the office, rights, or powers of another, without right or legal authority; one who takes possession of by force; one who takes arrogantly, as if by right.

magnitude of His victory will be made obvious in its completeness. So have confidence.

Stay close with each other and to me, my children. Know that I love you all and that I am the Mother, the true Mother of Perpetual Help. Good-bye.

MESSAGE FROM MARY
SEPTEMBER 20, 1995

My beautiful children, it is I, your Mother, who speaks with you this day as the Mother of Divine Protection. This protection is offered to you always. My arms are always open and near to you. My Jesus always answers a crying heart.

During these times, my children, the dark times when it appears the enemy has made such great inroads, remain strong in your faith. Respond to the beautiful grace that God has given you *to have faith in the Real Presence.*[114] Look lovingly upon Him with the eyes of the soul as often as possible, my children, for He feeds you and strengthens you.

I feel such pain for my children who reject this grace. They are left wandering in the desert, like the children of Israel so long ago. Without this gift of faith, they soon turn to revelry[115] and self-importance. As you see, my children, they even fashion God into images, created by human hands, that must fit their lifestyle, their desires, and their wants. It is this gift of faith that can allow my Son, the King of Kings, to enter your hearts and to protect you from all adventure.[116]

At the Holy Mass, be attentive to Him, worship Him, and in this way, let His light shine through you. It is a humble light. It is not prideful. It is not pushy. Concern yourself more with your interior motivations than the external actions of others. Grow in peace and love. Respond to His grace.

I love you all so much, my children. I ask you to continue your prayers for my intentions. *Know that the victory of my*

---

[114] **Real Presence:** The real presence of Jesus Christ in the Eucharist: body, blood, soul, and divinity

[115] The Bible uses this word to describe the Israelites' worship of the golden calf in Exodus 32.

[116] **Adventure:** a hazardous or perilous undertaking

Immaculate Heart is so very close. Have confidence. Have courage.

Good-bye, my children.

MESSAGE FROM MARY
SEPTEMBER 27, 1995

My beautiful children, it is I, your Mother, who speaks with you now. I come this day as the Queen of Peace,[117] so that I may settle your souls.

In this time of confusion and trial, when the enemy seems in control of almost every situation in your lives, know that I am with you. The enemy flees from my presence, and my peace will settle. That is the importance of these cenacles, my children—to come and enjoy this quiet and prayerful time so that your souls may be nourished and your hearts quieted by the Holy Spirit, Himself.

All crosses are heavy, my children. And I make you this promise that all of them will be lightened and your ability strengthened, if you persevere in your prayer, and ask, and love. Fear not Satan. I tell you, he flees from my presence. Have confidence in this.

I love you all so much, and I assure you my Son hears every prayer and suffers every pain with you. Far more important, my children, than a reduction in pain, is your progress in perfection. You all desire to be prepared for the Beatific Vision.[118] And it is for this purpose that I come.

I give you all my Maternal blessing and leave with a kiss. Good-bye.

---

[117] Queen of Peace: the title that Our Blessed Mother calls herself in Medjugorje

[118] **Beatific vision:** The inexpressible joy of Heaven consists, mysteriously, in the immediate vision of God. The Apostle John says: "My dear people, we are already children of God, but what we are to be in the future has not yet been revealed; all that we know is, that when it is revealed we shall be like Him because we shall see Him as He truly is" (1 Jn. 3:2). St. Paul writes: "Now we are seeing a dim reflection in a mirror; but then we shall be seeing face to face. The knowledge that I have now is imperfect; but then I shall know as fully as I am known" (1 Cor. 13:12). St. Gregory of Nyssa wrote: "The promise of seeing God surpasses all beatitude. . . In Scripture, to see is to possess. . . Whoever sees God has obtained all the goods of which he can conceive."

MESSAGE FROM MARY
OCTOBER 4, 1995

My beautiful children, it is I, your Mother, who speaks with you this day. It is good that you come to the presence of my Son, as He rests in the Tabernacle. His Heart mourns for His lost ones, and I cry tears, tears of suffering, for the pain that my lost children cause themselves and those around them. This suffering is the power of your prayers, my children, the power that heals. This is the path that all who wish to partake in the victory of my Immaculate Heart must walk.

Have confidence! . . . for my plan continues to unfold. My Son's Vicar[119] continues to teach, to evangelize, to proclaim the Gospel to a world grown cold and indifferent. Stay near him. Remain protected in his teaching. Know that in this way, you remain fully united to my Son. In this way, you come to know Him and love Him; in this way, you will find happiness. Be bold, confident, in spite of the signs you see about you. Have faith that the enemy's time is drawing swiftly to a climax.

My children, it is good that you come and pray together. My greatest desire is that you continue in this way. But do not leave the spirit here, my children. Take it with you into your work places, into your homes, into your circle of friends. Be discreet and loving. Avoid judgments and bitterness of feelings. I leave you now, but know that I pray for you and intercede for you constantly, and I will not cease until you are with me in the presence of God's glory.

Good-bye, my children.

---

119 Message given during the pontificate of Pope John Paul II

MESSAGE FROM MARY
OCTOBER 11, 1995

My beautiful and loving children, it is I, your Mother, and the Mother of your Lord who speaks with you this day. Let His peace fill your hearts. Become completely full of His love. He offers this to you every waking moment, and His angels guard you in your sleep.

The sign you seek is within you, my children. It is what draws you here week after week to pray for my holy intentions. I will tell you my intentions, children: they are to bring *all* to my Son. So simple. And as time passes, you will see how effective. Have confidence. Live the faith that has been given you from above. You are truly chosen—the elect. The sign of this is your faith.

When I say, "Have confidence, my children," be at peace with how the world reacts to events. Allow your lives to be shaped and molded in my hands. Fight for me and my plan with your prayers and the devotion of your hearts. Leave the rest to me. My children, it is enough that you perform your duties to the best of your abilities, that you pray and offer the sacrifice of the many disappointments in your lives. I have told you many times, these are flowers, beautiful flowers, that I make into a bouquet to lay at the feet of my Son.

Go now, my children, filled with the Spirit. I love you all, and I leave you now with my blessing. Good-bye.

MESSAGE FROM MARY
OCTOBER 18, 1995

My beautiful children, it is I, your Mother, who speaks with you this day. I am full of joy because of your many "yes's," your desire to please God, and your "oneness" with my Son. The secret to perseverance is prayer and the consistent receipt of the Sacraments. I implore you always to be conscious of this great gift. There lies all your strength and your ability.

Today I wish to speak to you with words of encouragement and consolation, for you engage in the great battle, the battle already won by my victorious Son. Be at peace and find strength in my arms. Know that the Father's plans for you will always progress towards ultimate good, if you continue to say "yes." Put aside your fears. Stay close to my heart, for in the closeness of the Immaculate Heart, you are "one" with my Son, for it is in my heart that He resides, abundantly and with grace overflowing for all of you.

I love you all, and I leave you with my consolation, in the knowledge that you make your Mother so joyful. Good-bye.

MESSAGE FROM MARY
OCTOBER 25, 1995

My beautiful children, how I love to be with you at these cenacles of prayer, my cenacles, through which this important plan of mine for you and those you touch is affected.

I embrace you. I call you to a special union with my Son, in the Immaculate Heart of His Mother. Here you will share His embrace . . . His loving and tender care. It girds and strengthens you for any trial or tribulation that may come your way. He is your solace and your shield, and He will never buckle, my children.

He loves you so. He watches over you and is with you every moment of the day. Every breath you take is a breath with Him. He truly lives in you, and you in Him. His grace is enough, my children. Be at peace in the Ark with my Son. Its destination is soon ahead. And the glory and the beauty that will be yours is worth any trial or torment that this life can force you to endure.

I thank you for your trust in me, for your love. Do not punish yourself for failures or slips. I am the Good Mother who patches all wounds, heals all maladies, and consoles all suffering hearts. Stay close to me, your Mother. I love you all, and I leave you now with my blessing and a promise from my Son to strengthen you for the work ahead. Good-bye, my children.

MESSAGE FROM MARY
NOVEMBER 1, 1995

My beautiful children, I am so happy to be with you this day. Oh, what a glorious day! The gates of heaven are opened for so many new saints who join in the new song, the hymn of victory.[120] The last stanza is soon to be sung, my children, and with it, my Son's glorious return.

Remain always vigilant. Reside in my Immaculate Heart with Him. You all bring Him your love in such a beautiful way at my cenacle. Your hearts soften, and you renew again your vows to avoid sin and to always please the Father. Cleanse and purify yourselves in the Sacraments. Let peace reign in your hearts, for that is where peace must begin. You will find it in no other way, my children.

You have many brothers and sisters,[121] holy and full of God's love. Their prayers with yours help so many. Some have reached their final purification this day and enter through the porthole of my Immaculate Heart, to be seated at the very throne of the Almighty. There they receive His blessings and His welcome into His glorious home.

In a special way this day, think of your brothers and sisters, of the joy they now have, and remember always: this is your final destination. This is where your journey leads. Pray for the grace of vigilance and strength. I pray every day for this for all of you in a very special way. The Sacrifice of my Son completed in my heart total love for each of you. Reside there and be happy.

---

[120] This day was All Saints' Day

[121] Our Lady refers to the Communion of Saints, which consists of the Church Triumphant in heaven, the Church Suffering in purgatory, and we, the Church Militant here on Earth.

I love you all, and I leave you with a Mother's blessing, as we await His joyous return and the vanquishment and destruction of the evil one. Good-bye, my children.

MESSAGE FROM MARY
NOVEMBER 8, 1995

Beautiful children of my cenacle, gather round me this day. Offer me your hearts so that I may clean them, purify them, and ready them for that unity of which I always speak—unity with my Son.

Through God's grace, you are always before the door, my children. In His providence, He sees to this. This is a special grace offered to all those who are near to me, who respond to my affection. But you must knock to enter in, my children. This entering is through a development of your interior life, a life of prayer and devotion to my Son, Jesus.

Don't be afraid, my children, for what you abandon is good to leave behind for the higher good. *You will find that through this intense interior life, this deep prayer, your responsibilities will be easier to fulfill and your work much more fruitful.* So I say again: be not afraid!

Come before my Son in a spirit of quiet and gentleness and humility. Open your heart completely to Him so that He may enter. He promises to fill. Oh, the joy of an interior life, my children! . . . *even* in this world. Come to me and I will help you. I will help to soften the wounds grown hard from indifference.

Be at peace, and know that I love you and that my Son forgives you. Good-bye.

MESSAGE FROM MARY
NOVEMBER 15, 1995

My children, it is I, your Mother, who speaks with you this day. It is a joy to be with you, to be present so that you may gather in my arms and find rest in the oasis of my Immaculate Heart.

There, I cleanse and soften your wounds, the wounds that make your likeness compare to my Son. These are the wounds you must cultivate, my children—the wounds you suffer for God and for your brothers and sisters. Through prayer and interior life, you will come to learn the wounds that you share with my Son are different from the wounds that are self-inflicted, or that burn at pride and intolerance. Have confidence that I, your Mother, will help you with this.

Know that when you pray, I am always with you, for solace and support. Exalt in the wounds you share with my Son, for they bring you closer to the Father. And know that if you endure, your place will be an exalted one in the Father's house. You are engaged in such a great work, my children. The efficaciousness of your prayers you will only learn much later. They have a great role. They are very important to me. In spite of dryness, I plead with you to persevere in this prayer.

God bless you all. I love you now. . . I love you always. Be at peace. Good-bye.

MESSAGE FROM MARY
NOVEMBER 29, 1995

Oh, my children, it is I, your Mother, who speaks with you this day—the Mother of All the Living. And I ask for your continued support of my cenacle and its mission. Please know, my children, you participate in a very real way in the important work of my plan. Be not troubled, for it is my work. Have confidence in my Immaculate Heart.

Know that in your smallness, your nothingness before God, His mercy may fill you. The proud and the haughty may talk of His mercy, but they will know it not. Know that I lead you through the darkness by the strength of my intercession, united with your prayers. The beacon, the lighted path, is my Son and His way.

I ask your help, my children, through continued prayer and sacrifice and confidence in me, your Mother. Nothing will change in the Father's plan. Remain in my arms, enveloped in the love of my Immaculate and Sorrowful Heart that prays for you always.[122] Be at peace, my children. Allow my plan to unfold. Participate through prayer and the activities presented to you. Ask for God's strength. Remain always in generosity and love towards one another.

I love you all so much. I leave you now with a tender caress and an interior knowing[123] of a Mother's love. Good-bye.

---

[122] At the end of each cenacle Rosary, the members would say: "Immaculate and Sorrowful Heart of Mary, pray for us." Our Blessed Mother was responding to our petition.

[123] This day during the Rosary, many in the cenacle received the gift of tears. Perhaps this is what Our Blessed Mother is referring to when she said that they were given "an interior knowing of a Mother's love."

MESSAGE FROM MARY
DECEMBER 6, 1995

My beautiful children, it is I, your Mother, who speaks with you this day. I thank you for your perseverance . . . your continued presence in my cenacle. It is in my cenacle that you are fully wrapped in my mantle, protected from the pressures and anxieties of the world, and given respite from the temptations of the evil one. Enjoy this rest, my children, for soon you must go out and face all these trials.

I know, my children, it is so difficult at times. I weep for you, and I pray. In times of darkness and severe trial, call out my name. If you do this in humility, the Father always responds. He sends me with a Mother's help to bring back His lost little ones. No matter how dark or how deep, I always find them.

In any circumstance you find yourself, please call me by name, and I will be there. My arms are a sure refuge. There you will find strength. There you will find all you need, for as you rest in my arms, the Sacred Heart of my Son envelopes you, molds you, into the beautiful child of God you were meant to be.

Know that when your weakness is shown to you, it is done for the purpose of pointing out to you that you must have confidence only in God, for He is strength and He is your purpose, always. Good-bye, my children. Know that I love you and place your petitions at the feet of my Son . . . every day. Good-bye.

MESSAGE FROM MARY
DECEMBER 20, 1995

My beautiful children, it is I, your Mother, who speaks with you this day. Be at peace. Know that Love is at hand.[124] We soon commemorate the greatest event in the history of creation, the Incarnation—the coming of God into His creation to sanctify it with His eternal and sublime love, a love of sacrifice that knows no limits, my children.

A spirit of false humility attacks so many hearts at this time. It seeks to convince them that they are not worthy. They ask: "Why would God condescend[125] to take on our form?" What a terrible mistake, my children, for a heart to be convinced that its littleness is preeminent and more significant than God's limitless love. He became Man to bring each of you home, and this He will do . . . in time, my children.

Be at peace. Continue your prayers and supplications.[126] I use these directly for my work in your local church and in many areas of such urgent need. Hold fast and be strong. I will never abandon you. Good-bye, my children.

---

[124] Our Blessed Mother, like John the Baptist, announces that the coming of Our Lord is near.

[125] **Condescend:** to agree to do something one considers beneath one's dignity or rank

[126] **Supplications:** humble and earnest requests of God through prayer; an earnest appeal

MESSAGE FROM MARY
DECEMBER 27, 1995

My beautiful children, I am so happy to be with you this day, especially since it follows so closely the celebration of the birth of my Son and Our Lord. Those days following His birth were so serene and peaceful. The world knew Him not, save for those chosen souls who were blessed by the angels.

They received Him in faith, though He could not have been in a more lowly position. He was wrapped in the clothing of poverty—food for the salvation of man, laid in a manger for animals. This was not without purpose, my children, for God Who is mighty does great things for us all, and in His incomprehensible way, shows us the preeminence of humility and faith. It is the gift of faith that the shepherds responded to, and it is this gift that you are all asked to respond to.

I tell you, this is truly the time of God's mercy, my Son's mercy, and it will remain so until He comes in glory for the time of justice. Stay awake in your hearts, my children. Try always to be ready for Him. When you fall, allow me to pick you up and bring you back to the fold.

Be at peace, and know that I share my love with you. Good-bye.

MESSAGE FROM MARY
JANUARY 3, 1996

My beautiful children, I thank you for coming together to pray, to share in the grace and the blessings open to all those who come to my cenacle.

In preparation for the Epiphany, I ask you to contemplate the Infant Child Jesus, the King of Kings, my beautiful Son, as He lay in poverty. God reveals Himself to the humble, be they rich or poor. It is through humility that God reaches hearts. I implore you, my children, always place my Son before your worldly desires. And since you do not see my Son, how do you do this? You do see Him, my children, for He is in each of you. Put each other first, and I promise you riches and glory beyond comprehension.

Resist the temptations that always come before you. The enemy tries so very hard, my children, to dissuade you, to discourage you—especially in discouragement—for it is here that he hides his true plans for you. I love you all so much, and I offer you the comfort of a Mother's arms. No matter your moods, no matter the feelings that push and prod at you, remember you are always and at all times welcome in my arms. Be at peace, my children. I leave you now with my blessing. Good-bye.

MESSAGE FROM MARY
JANUARY 10, 1996

My beautiful children, I am so happy to be here with you this day to pray with you. This is a great blessing that heaven condescends to give you, my children. Praying together as one family brings my Son so very close.

At this time, especially, beware of discouragement, the enemy's tricks and wiles. As you strive for perfection, the world *will* weigh you down, my children. Know that I am with you to help you. My Son offered to carry this burden for you, and He will. But as you strive, look to find the perfection within yourselves and those whom you love. Do this, rather than seeking perfection from them.

If you find yourself unable to pray or to fulfill the commitments you've made, know that I love you and that my Son loves you. Pick yourself up and continue. Be not afraid, my children, for either yourselves or your loved ones, for they are under my Maternal care. My Son is the Good Shepherd, and He does not easily lose His sheep.

Find peace in my words, my children. Know that my work does not abate. It is now continuing and building momentum. These times are glorious. Have confidence in this. I give you my blessing, and I leave you now with my kiss of tenderness and Motherly compassion. Good-bye.

MESSAGE FROM MARY
JANUARY 24, 1996

Most beautiful children of God, it is I, your Mother, the Mother of Perpetual Help, who speaks with you this day. I give you my peace, children—a peace that will carry you through these tumultuous times.

Pray always that the Father's will be done. Know that my plan depends on the action of the Holy Spirit in all my children's souls. Remain confident that your Mother knows what's best for all her children and will never abandon them.

I thank you for your perseverance. I know the trials you suffer. The cross is always very painful. But it is through the cross that all learn to love, for in the Cross, my Son—the Love of the World—immolated Himself to the Father. When you do the same, my children, you enter into His Cross, and that sacrifice is most pleasing.

I love you all, and I pray that you will remain strong in the face of those forces that wish to destroy all that is beautiful, all that is glorious. Remain steadfast, my children, and know that the victory will soon be here. Good-bye.

MESSAGE FROM MARY
FEBRUARY 7, 1996

My beautiful children, it is I, your Mother, who speaks with you this day, and I come to you as your Mother of Tender Mercy. Rest in my arms. Find solace in my words of love and encouragement. Be at peace and resign yourselves to God's holy will. I assure you, God will provide, my children, the strength you need to persevere in your work, to suffer the trials and privations that life brings your way.

To suffer all this in union with my Son is a great gift, for in this you *are* united to my Son and His Sacrifice. Offer all your sufferings and trials, great and small, to His Cross, for there is great merit in this, especially those sufferings you endure for the Faith, my children . . . for when you suffer for the Faith, you suffer for the children of God, and no greater love does any person have.

Your work is my work. It is a seed given you to plant, to nourish, and to guard. But who makes it grow, my children? Not your labors—only the grace of God. And though it may seem to die, it will grow into beautiful flowers. The bloom will be seen by many of God's children and bring much joy. Have confidence and persevere. Suffer all trials with dignity and repose, and recognize God's work.

I love you all so much, and I am so proud at the way you have carried my banner. You will not fail, my children, if you remain in prayer . . . and in my joy. Resign yourselves again to God's holy will, and find peace in this. Good-bye, my beautiful children.

MESSAGE FROM MARY
FEBRUARY 21, 1996

My beautiful and loving children, it is a great blessing from God that I am here with you this day.[127] Be at peace. Calm your hearts. Know that I love you dearly. Each of you is a special child of mine.

Satan has boasted that he could scatter you to the four winds, and I am so pleased that he has failed.[128] Maintain your confidence in me and in my plan. It is a small and humble plan, a plan of preparation, a plan of victory. This victory is the victory of my Immaculate Heart—to preserve the Church and save souls for my Son. He has deemed this for this time, the time of false doctrine, a time as prophesied, when the true doctrines would be ignored, blasphemed, and ridiculed.

Don't fear. Reside *in* my heart and know that there you will find safe refuge. As my Son's victory over death was seen by the world as a defeat, so will my victory be, my children. So do not look as the world looks. Look with the interior eyes that have been a gift to you from the Thrice Holy God. Remain steadfast. Remain confident because you are united with my heart.

I love you all so much, and I leave you with my Maternal kiss of peace, love, and an interior joy. Good-bye.

---

[127] Ash Wednesday

[128] This week was a time of great temptation for some individuals to give up on the work they had been doing in the diocese.

MESSAGE FROM MARY
FEBRUARY 28, 1996

Beautiful children of God, it is I, your Mother, who speaks with you this day. I come to you as the Mother of Lost Children. With me this day is my beautiful Infant, the Lord of Lords and the King of Kings. I bring Him this day so you may be blessed by His presence, and so your hearts may be warmed by the knowledge of His love.

My message is simple and clear, my children. It is my Son's message. It is the message that brings light to the world. As bearers of this message, those who do evil and live in darkness find in you criticism and accusation. This is because the light is painful to their choice, my children. But do not despair, for my Son's message is only received by those who have eyes to see and ears to hear. This is a grace of God that comes and goes with the Holy Spirit. That is where I want you to be concerned, my children. That's where your prayers must be . . . with those who make choices.

Why do I come this day as the Mother of Lost Children? It is to give you confidence that those in darkness, those who suffer pain, scandal, and torture, are in my prayers and in my devotions. Jesus knows they are mine, and I will bring them back in time. For now, have confidence in me as your Mother.

Be at peace. This peace I talk of is not a feeling, but rather an interior understanding, a knowing that you are in God's will . . . you work within the parameters He has set for you. *This* is the peace I talk of. In this peace, my children, there is still pain and sorrow. There is still at times frustration. But you may pray at all times for strength to resist the temptations of the devil, because my Son is always near. Be obedient, my children. If you do not find this peace I describe in your obedience, know that it is because pride, that terrible demon, is lurking so near.

I love you all, and I long for the day I may hold you in my arms, as I do my beautiful and Infant Son. Good-bye.

MESSAGE FROM MARY
MARCH 6, 1996

Beautiful children of the Father, I come this day as your loving Mother, the Mother of Your Redemption. Do not fear the evil one, for my Son has paid the price. There is nothing that he can do to harm you, unless you allow it freely. The harm I speak of is eternal harm.

In a special way, I touch your hearts this day and give you my blessing. I wish you to know that heaven rejoices at your prayers and sacrifices—the big ones and the most humble. Remember always, my children, that small and little penances completed are far more valuable than great ones abandoned. Humility will help you to recognize this, my children, so that you may remain steadfast in all you undertake.

I love you all so much, and I leave you with my tender embrace. Good-bye.

MESSAGE FROM MARY
MARCH 13, 1996

My beautiful children, I come to you today as the Mother of Truth, and that Truth is my Son. During this time, as you prepare for His glorious rise, find peace with yourself and with your loved ones. I ask each of you to do this.

The devil causes so much strife and pain, and he finds easy access to so many because of their lack of humility. The evil one cannot abide long where there is this great virtue, my children. *But humility is not weak.* It is a strong virtue, and it is largely a gift of the Spirit. But in all of you, children, make it habitual, for as you work, as you strive to increase the size of your reservoir, the Holy Spirit will fill it. Every time you lose your temper, every time you grow arrogant or prideful, you fill in your reservoir and reduce its capacity.

Remain resolute, my children. Know that there is great merit in your efforts. Find joy in your successes, and know that when you do fall, I am there to gather you in my arms. My arms are a great place of rest. I assure you, my children, if my Son could find respite from the world there, so will you.

Go in peace with my love. Good-bye.

MESSAGE FROM MARY
MARCH 27, 1996

My beautiful children, I come to you this day as the Mother of All Charity. The Divine Love is All in all, and a spark of this Love is in each of you. You must kindle this spark until it becomes a roaring flame. This is the flame I ask of you to share in. This is the flame that will bring all of God's children back to the fold. But you build this flame one stick— one tinder—at a time, my children.

You apply the abundant graces that God bestows on you. This application must begin in your homes. This is where your prayer lives must develop. This is one of the secret rooms that my Son talks of. Whether you are a family of one with me and my Son and the Father and the Spirit, or a family of many, is not what is important. What is important, again, is the building and sharing of charity, trust, and forgiveness.

There is no pain so great that you are not called to forgive, my children, for my Son forgives and He forgets. And you are called to forget. I love you all so much. There is so much I wish to share with you, to teach you in the ways of charity. This I have done, and this I will continue to do, as I gather you about me. But don't grasp at this, my children. Don't allow the devil's covetousness to trap you. Share what I give you. Remain obedient to the law of charity. Good-bye.

MESSAGE FROM MARY
APRIL 3, 1996
HOLY WEEK

My beloved children, sons and daughters of God, I come to form you, to help you on the right path, that path that is so narrow and full of obstacles.

I wish this day to share with you a great secret . . . a secret that will help you. It is talked about much, but few understand it. This secret of which I speak is a simple examination of conscience. The daily trials you undergo, the storms that whip at you are, in many cases, designed by the evil one to weaken your resolve.

This is why examination is so important . . . for together with the Sacraments and a deep prayer life, this examination will help you to ferret out God's will from the enemy's. He disguises himself and works through your imagination and your emotions so that you become confused. The waters are muddied . . . your vision unclear.

But if you observe this simple principle I give you, perform it faithfully, my children, you will grow much closer to me and to my Son. And as you empty yourself of selfish motives, my Son will fill you, and you will become His living presence, His light that shines.

Find comfort in my words, my children. Know that I love and support you always. My prayers are for your success, that the journey may be safe, and that you may come home without harm.

Good-bye.

MESSAGE FROM MARY
APRIL 17, 1996

Children of God, I come to you today as the Mother of Consolation—the only true consolation, my Son. Jesus is the answer, my children. It is Him you must continually seek in the world, in each other, and in yourselves.

Remain steadfast and obedient. The Church is a great gift, my children. Listen to her. Mind her ways. Let peace reign in your hearts.

The Father has graciously given you to me to form. I hold each of you in my arms, consoling and caressing, molding you to be the true children that I want you to be. I always lead to the Trinity those children given to me for this purpose.

Please remain a beautiful family. Avoid dissension. Remain steadfast. My mantle of protection will always surround you. I implore you to persevere in your prayer as a sign to the world of my maternal blessing.

This is my time, and my plan is unfolding. Be at peace with all that transpires. Have confidence in me. I love you all so much, and I wish that all of you remain so close—so familial that your prayers come as one to the Father through my beloved cenacle.

Good-bye, my children. Know that I am with you always.

FINAL MESSAGE FROM JESUS

Children of God, it is I, your Lord and Savior, Who speaks with you now. You must take My Mother's words and ponder them in your heart. There, they will assist you to grow into the flames of charity I wish you all to be. Only in this way will you assist Me in filling heaven with souls, beautiful souls created from the beginning to be with Me. Resist temptations to despair, and listen to My Mother, for these are the times that I speak through her.

Notes to the Reader

AMAZON REVIEWS

If you were graced by this book, would you kindly post a short review of *She Who Shows the Way* on Amazon.com? Your support will make a difference in the lives of souls and our future.

To leave a short review, go to Amazon.com and type in *She Who Shows the Way.* Click on the book and scroll down the page. Next to customer reviews, click on "Write a customer review." Thank you, in advance, for your kindness.

MORE MESSAGES FROM HEAVEN

If you are interested in learning more about what Our Lord and Our Lady are purportedly saying to the world for our times, see: www.CountdowntotheKingdom.com.

NEWSLETTER

Sign up for the Queen of Peace Media monthly newsletter to be informed of resources to help you navigate these tumultuous times.
www.QueenofPeaceMedia.com/newsletter

OTHER BOOKS
BY THE AUTHOR

Libros disponible en español

www.queenofpeacemedia.com/libreria-catolica

EL AVISO
Testimonios y Profecías de la Iluminación de Conciencia

EL MANTO DE MARÍA
Una Consagración Mariana para Ayuda Celestial

EL MANTO DE MARÍA
Diario de Oración para la Consagración

TRANSFIGURADA
La Historia de Patricia Sandoval

HOMBRES JUNTO A MARÍA
Así Vencieron Seis Hombres la Más Ardua Batalla
de Sus Vidas

THE WARNING

TESTIMONIES AND PROPHECIES OF
THE ILLUMINATION OF CONSCIENCE
with *IMPRIMATUR*

en español:
EL AVISO

Endorsed by Bishop Gavin Ashenden, Msgr. Ralph J. Chieffo, Fr. John Struzzo, Mark Mallet, Fr. Berdardin Mugabo, and more…

Includes the fascinating story of Marino Restrepo, hailed as a St. Paul for our century

(See www.queenofpeacemedia.com/the-warning for the book trailer)

The Warning has been an Amazon #1 best-seller, ever since its release. In the book are authentic accounts of saints and mystics of the Church who have spoken of a day when we will all see our souls in the light of truth, and fascinating stories of those who have already experienced it for themselves.

"With His divine love, He will open the doors of hearts and illuminate all consciences. Every person will see himself in the burning fire of divine truth. It will be like a judgment in miniature."

—Our Lady to Fr. Stefano Gobbi of the Marian Movement of Priests

#1 AMAZON BEST-SELLER

IMPRIMATUR FROM ARCHBISHOP-EMERITUS RAMÓN C. ARGÜELLES, STL

THE WARNING
TESTIMONIES AND PROPHECIES OF
THE ILLUMINATION OF CONSCIENCE

#1 BEST SELLER

"Tremendous... Invaluable."
—Mark Mallett

"This book should be widely disseminated, all for God's glory."
—Archbishop-Emeritus Ramón C. Argüelles, STL

"Read this prophetic book and believe."
—Msgr. Ralph J. Chieffo

Includes the story of Marino Restrepo, hailed as a St. Paul for our century

CHRISTINE WATKINS
Forward by Bishop Gavin Ashenden

264

OF MEN AND MARY

HOW SIX MEN WON THE GREATEST BATTLE OF THEIR LIVES

"Of Men and Mary is superb. The six life testimonies contained within it are miraculous, heroic, and truly inspiring."
— **Fr. Gary Thomas**
Pastor, exorcist, and subject of the book and movie, "The Rite."

"Anointed!"
— **Fr. Donald Calloway, MIC**
(See www.queenofpeacemedia.com/of-men-and-mary
For the book trailer and to order)

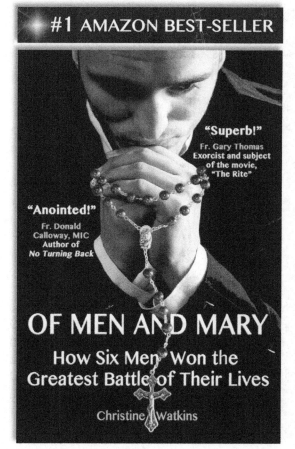

Turn these pages, and you will find yourself surprisingly inspired by a murderer locked up in prison, a drug-using football player who dreamed of the pros, and a selfish, womanizing daredevil who died and met God. You will root for a husband and father whose marriage was a battleground, a man searching desperately to belong, pulled by lust and illicit attractions, and an innocent lamb who lost, in a single moment, everyone he cared about most. And you will rejoice that their sins and their pasts were no obstacle for heaven.

FULL OF GRACE

MIRACULOUS STORIES OF HEALING AND CONVERSION THROUGH MARY'S INTERCESSION

"Christine Watkins's beautiful and touching collection of conversion stories are direct, honest, heart-rending, and miraculous."

—**Wayne Weible**
Author of *Medjugorje: The Message*

(See www.queenofpeacemedia.com/full-of-grace for the book trailer and to order)

In this riveting book, Christine Watkins tells her dramatic story of miraculous healing and conversion to Catholicism, along with the stories of five others: a homeless drug addict, an altar boy trapped by cocaine, a stripper, a lonely youth, and a modern-day hero.

Following each story is a message that Mary has given to the world. And for those eager to probe the deeper, reflective waters of discipleship—either alone or within a prayer group—a Scripture passage, prayerful reflection questions, and a spiritual exercise at the end of each chapter offer an opportunity to enliven our faith.

TRANSFIGURED

PATRICIA SANDOVAL'S STORY

Endorsed by
**Archbishop Salvatore Cordileone & Bishop Michael Barber, SJ,
and Fr. Donald Calloway, MIC**

**Disponible También en Español: TRANSFIGURADA
avalado por EMMANUEL**

**(See www.queenofpeacemedia.com/transfigured
for the book trailer, the companion DVD, and to order)**

"Are you ready to read one of the most powerful conversion stories ever written? Seriously, are you? It's a bold and shocking claim, I admit. But the story you are about to have the pleasure of reading is so intense and brutally candid that I wouldn't be surprised if it brings you to tears multiple times and opens the door to an experience of mercy and healing. This story is made for the big screen, and I pray it makes it there someday. It's that incredible. . . What you are about to read is as raw, real, and riveting as a story can get. I couldn't put this book down!"

**—Fr. Donald Calloway,
MIC**
Author of
Consecration to St. Joseph
and *No Turning Back*

MARY'S MANTLE CONSECRATION

A SPIRITUAL RETREAT FOR HEAVEN'S HELP

Disponible también en español—*El Manto de María: Una Consagración Mariana para Ayuda Celestial*

Endorsed by **Archbishop Salvatore Cordileone** and **Bishop Myron J. Cotta**

(See www.MarysMantleConsecration.com to see a video of amazing testimonies and to order)

"I am grateful to Christine Watkins for making this disarmingly simple practice, which first grew in the fertile soil of Mexican piety, available to the English-speaking world."
—**Archbishop Salvatore Cordileone**

"Now more than ever, we need a miracle. Christine Watkins leads us through a 46-day self-guided retreat that focuses on daily praying of the Rosary, a Little fasting, and meditating on various virtues and the seven gifts of the Holy Spirit, leading to a transformation in our lives and in the people on the journey with us!"
—**Fr. Sean O. Sheridan, TOR**
Former President, Franciscan University of Steubenville

MARY'S MANTLE CONSECRATION

PRAYER JOURNAL
to accompany the consecration book

Disponible también en español—
El Manto de Maria: Diario de Oración para la Consagración

PREPARE FOR AN OUTPOURING
OF GRACE UPON YOUR LIFE

**(See www.MarysMantleConsecration.com
to see a video of amazing testimonies and to order)**

St. Pope John Paul II said that his consecration to Mary was "a decisive turning point in my life." It can be the same for you.

This *Prayer Journal* with daily Scriptures, saint quotes, questions for reflection and space for journaling is a companion book to the popular *Mary's Mantle Consecration*, a self-guided retreat that has resulted in miracles in the lives and hearts of those who have applied themselves to it. This prayer journal will take you even deeper into your soul and into God's transforming grace.

WINNING THE BATTLE FOR YOUR SOUL

JESUS' TEACHINGS THROUGH MARINO RESTREPO, A ST. PAUL FOR OUR CENTURY

Endorsed by Archbishop-Emeritus, Ramón C. Argüelles
"This book is an authentic jewel of God!"
—Internationally renowned author, María Vallejo-Nájera
(See <u>The Warning: Testimonies and Prophecies of the Illumination of Conscience</u> to read Marino's testimony)

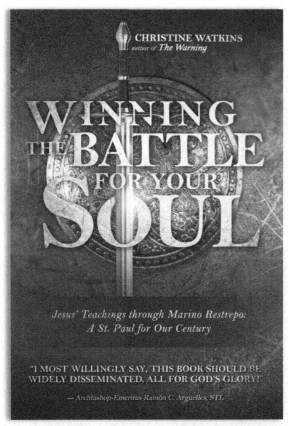

Marino Restrepo was a sinful man kidnapped for ransom by Colombian terrorists and dragged into the heart of the Amazon jungle. In the span of just one night, the Lord gave him an illumination of his conscience followed by an extraordinary infusion of divine knowledge. Today, Marino is hailed as one of the greatest evangelizers of our time.

In addition to giving talks around the world, Marino is the founder of the Church-approved apostolate, Pilgrims of Love.

This little book contains some of the most extraordinary teachings that Jesus has given to the world through Marino Restrepo, teachings that will profoundly alter and inform the way you see your ancestry, your past, your purpose, your future, and your very salvation.

IN LOVE WITH TRUE LOVE

THE UNFORGETTABLE STORY OF SISTER NICOLINA

(See www.QueenofPeaceMedia.com and Amazon.com)

In this seemingly loveless world of ours, we might wonder if true love is attainable. Is it real, or is it perhaps a dancing illusion captured on Hollywood screens? And if this love dares to exist, does it satisfy as the poets say, or fade in our hearing like a passing whisper?

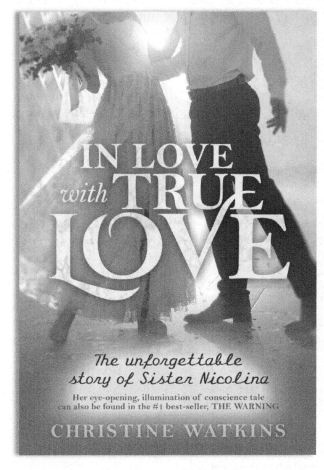

The souls are few who have discovered these answers, and one of them is Nicolina, a feisty, flirtatious girl who fell in love with the most romantic man in all of post-war Germany.

Little did they imagine the places where love would take them.

This enthralling, real-life short story is a glimpse into the grand secrets of true love—secrets that remain a conundrum to most, but become life itself for a grateful few. These hidden treasures wait in hope to be discovered, resting in chambers of the Heart of Love. Through this little book, may you, like Nicolina, enter their mystery, and find life, too.

MARIE-JULIE JAHENNY

PROPHECIES AND PROTECTION
FOR THE END TIMES

(See www.QueenofPeaceMedia.com. Soon on Amazon.com)

Marie-Julie Jahenny (1850-1941) is one of the most extraordinary mystics in the history of the Church. This humble peasant from devout parents in Britanny, France, received numerous visitations from heaven and lived with multiple wounds of the stigmata for most of her long life.

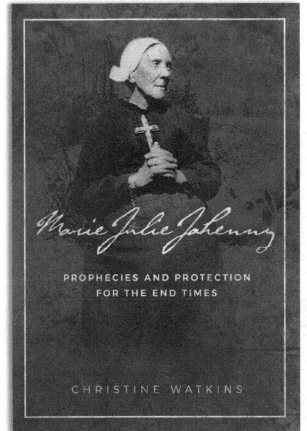

Jahenny's selfless spirit endures as a gift to the Church, for she received knowledge of what lies on the horizon of our current era.

Jahenny was supported by her local bishop, Msgr. Fournier of Nantes, who said of her, "I see nothing but good."

In addition to Jahenny's special mission from the Lord to spread the love of the Cross, she was called to prepare the world for the coming chastisements, which precede and prepare the world for the glorious renewal of Christendom in the promised era of peace.

Through Marie-Julie, the Lord has given help, remedies, and protection for the times we now live in, and those soon to come. As Christ said to her on several occasions, "I want My people to be warned."

PURPLE SCAPULAR

OF BLESSING AND PROTECTION
FOR THE END TIMES

**Jesus and Mary have given this scapular to the world
for our times!**

Go to **www.queenofpeacemedia.com/product/purple-scapular-of-blessing-and-protection** to read about all of the incredible promises given to those who wear it in faith.

Our Lady's words to the mystic, stigmatist, and victim soul, Marie-Julie Jahenny: "My children, all souls, all people who possesses this scapular will see their family protected. Their home will also be protected, **foremost from fires**. . . for a long time my Son and I have had the desire to make known this scapular of benediction...

This first apparition of this scapular will be a new protection for the times of the chastisements, of the calamities, and the famines. All those who are clothed (with it) shall pass under the storms, the tempests, and the darkness. They will have light as if it were plain day. Such is the power of this unknown scapular..."

273

THE FLAME OF LOVE

THE SPIRITUAL DIARY
OF ELIZABETH KINDELMANN

(See www.QueenofPeaceMedia.com/flame-love-love-book-bundle)

Extraordinary graces of literally blinding Satan, and reaching heaven quickly are attached to the spiritual practices and promises in this spiritual classic. On August 2, 1962, Our Lady said these remarkable words to mystic and victim soul, Elizabeth Kindelmann:

"Since the Word became Flesh, I have never given such a great movement as the Flame of Love that comes to you now. Until now, there has been nothing that so blinds Satan."

THE FLAME OF LOVE

In this special talk, Christine Watkins introduces the Flame of Love of the Immaculate Heart of Mary.

This worldwide movement in the Catholic Church is making true disciples of Jesus Christ in our turbulent times and preparing souls for the Triumph of Our Lady's Heart and the New Pentecost.

See www.ChristineWatkins.com.
Email cwatkins@queenofpeacemedia.com.

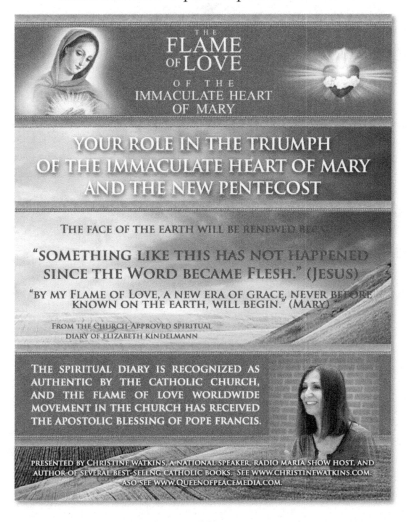

Queen of Peace
MEDIA
.com

Made in the USA
Coppell, TX
25 November 2020

42030474R00154